A Journey Away from

MW01062969

Why
Surrender
is NOT a
Four Letter Word

LINDA RUSSELL

ACW Press
Ozark, AL 36360

Cover Design by Alpha Advertising
Interior Design by Pine Hill Graphics

Packaged by ACW Press
1200 HWY 231 South #273
Ozark, AL 36360
www.acwpress.com
The views expressed or implied in this work do not necessarily reflect those of ACW Press. Ultimate design, content, and editorial accuracy of this work is the responsibility of the author(s).

Library of Congress Cataloging-in-Publication Data
(Provided by Cassidy Cataloguing Services, Inc.)

Russell, Linda Kay.

　Why surrender is not a four-letter word / Linda Kay Russell. -- 1st ed. -- Ozark, AL : ACW Press, 2005.

　　p. ; cm.

　　Includes bibliographical references.
　　ISBN: 1-932124-60-8

　　1. Theological virtues. 2. Christian life. 3. Faith.
　　I. Title.

BV4635 .R87 2005
241/.4--dc22   0505

Printed in the United States of America.

Contents

Acknowledgements

This book has truly been an incredible journey of love. God pursued, planted the seed, and carried me through to the end. That He would use me in such a way still amazes me, my family, and my friends.

First, and foremost, I thank God for allowing me the honor and privilege of sharing this story of His love with you. It has been a labor of love.

To my dearest friend, Marsha—I am daily blessed by her friendship, support, editing, tireless encouragement, and, yes, even her tender admonishments, when my warped sense of humor got out of control.

To my family, I am thankful for their support and generous words of encouragement. They are my life; they are my joy; they are God's blessed gift to me.

Finally, thanks to my many friends who took the time to read and offer much appreciated, and honest, feedback.

I am certain none of these people really understand their contribution to the completion of this book. I would have never considered myself capable of such a daunting task and was certain God had called upon the wrong person. Prior to this, I had never completed anything I had started. The negative voices chanting my theme song, "You'll never be good enough; you'll never be smart enough; add this to the long list of things you will never finish," were loud and clear right from the start. But, two things drown them out: my sense of God's continued presence through the entire process, and the unrelenting cheering of my precious family and friends. I have been blessed beyond measure, and I can never thank them enough.

Introduction

A Whale Of A Story

Jonah is reclining in his favorite chair, watching reruns of "Survivor" (probably thinking he missed his calling). God speaks to him. His instructions are short and to the point, "Get up and go tell the people of Nineveh I'm sick of their wickedness and pagan practices. This is an ultimatum—either turn or burn!" And Jonah's response? "Ain't no way. I'm outta here." Did he *say* that to God? No. Actually, he didn't say anything. He just got up, left the TV blaring, left dinner on the stove, and ran to the first ship heading out of port.

At 2:00 in the morning, watching my little MG being pulled from a muddy cornfield, I can assure you, I wasn't thinking about Jonah. I wasn't thinking about him two years later, behind the wheel of that same car—drunk, and praying for an encounter with an immovable object. As a matter of fact, for the better part of my life, he never crossed my mind. Like most people I never actually gave him serious thought—until I began this book. As I read the book of Jonah, again, I have come to believe for the first time that we must be kindred spirits.

Many people tend to brush off Jonah's story as nothing more than a tall tale. It is just a flash of God's humor. But, if that were true, how is it that Jesus told the Pharisees and Scribes about Jonah in Matthew 12:40? "*For as Jonah was three days and three nights in the belly of the great fish, so will the Son of Man be three days and three nights in the heart of the earth.*"[1]

Jonah's story is rich in substance and abounding in life's lessons. So much so, that I have chosen to use it to introduce you to the purpose and content of the book you now hold in your hands. Jonah and I are going to travel together through Galatians 5:22,23, the *Fruits of the Spirit, "But the fruit of the Spirit is love, joy, peace, longsuffering, kindness, goodness, faithfulness, gentleness, self-control..."*[2]

Galatians tells us, "If we live in the Spirit, let us also walk in the Spirit."[3] That to me, in a word, means surrender. It means I am supposed to live my life being loving, joyful, peaceful, longsuffering, kind, good, faithful, gentle, and self-controlled. There is simply no way that would be humanly possible. I know—I tried. It is only with God's grace and tender mercy that I have been able to overcome a life of immense hurt and the pain of sin and self-centeredness. I am not going to tell you here, or at the end of this book, that I live those virtues perfectly. It is a daily process. It is a daily decision to surrender my will to God's. Some days it is easy, and some days hiding in the belly of a whale doesn't seem like such a bad idea.

As for Jonah, sadly, I'm not sure he ever got it. He tested God's resolve and God made fish food out of him. Over the years, I too have tested God's resolve and have tried to hide from him. Do you know how silly that is? Let me give you an illustration. My three-year-old grandson, Noah, loves to play hide-and-seek. Last week we were playing and I was "it." As I was counting to ten, he searched for a place to hide. He grabbed a basket, put it over his head, and stood in the middle of the room giggling. When I opened my eyes I could not control my laughter. He was convinced I couldn't see him. That's how effective Jonah and I were at hiding. Perhaps Jonah continued to run the rest of his life, and there's no indication that God ever used him again. So, that's where our spirits part company.

For me, it has been a long road from despair and near suicide to a life God has graced—from a sense that I was unworthy of love, to the realization that God's love knows no bounds. Only the cross could reflect that love which human understanding fails to grasp. When Jesus surrendered, He didn't just give up owning a condo at the lake, cursing in front of the kids, or holding onto resentments. He gave up his life. His *life!* Do you see it? Do you see that sacrifice each time you look at the cross? Did Jonah? Sacrificing pride and arrogance was too much to ask of Jonah. What is God asking you to sacrifice? Is it worth it? I believe it is and I am praying that my story speaks to that belief. Thank you for allowing me the privilege of sharing it with you.

May God richly bless you,

Linda

Chapter One

LOVE

"We love Him because He first loved us."[1]

Aha love. I used to believe that love was connected to my physical appearance. Most of my life I considered myself ugly and fat, therefore undesirable and unlovable. How about you? Do you know what *real* love is?

The world's definition can include anything we want it to. We might love mint chocolate chip ice cream, our new car, or even shopping. It can be humorous, as we watch Miss Piggy float across a field of flowers: heart beating wildly, knees weak, stomach all a-flutter, "Ohhhhhhh Kermie!" It can come with no expectations or commitments: "I use to love you when you were thin and had more hair," "I could have loved you until your ex-wife got all your money," "You didn't tell me I had to love your kids too!" It is depicted in the lyrics, "I said I loved you, but I lied." How about this classic love ballad? Come on sing along with me—you know the words, "If you can't be with the one you love, love the one you're with."

Love can be abusive and demanding: parents abuse, women control, men lust—all in the name of love. Worldly love wears the sheep skin of an "if it feels good" mentality over the wolf that devours childhood innocence, destroys relationships, makes compassion a burden, and muddies the pure waters of selfless love created by God. As long as we seek love from things of this world we will always come up a little more lost and a little emptier for the effort. The lie perpetuates the madness.

How is God's love different? Let's read from 1 Corinthians 13 together. Stop me when we get to a part that matches the world's view. *"Love suffers long and is kind; love does not envy; love does not parade itself, is not puffed up; does not behave rudely, does not seek its own, is not provoked, thinks no evil; does not rejoice in iniquity, but rejoices in the truth; bears all things, believes all things, hopes all things, endures all things."* What happened? You didn't stop me. Why? Because God's love and the world's love are, well—worlds apart.

No one said God's way was easy. The Bible depicts a love uncharacteristic of the world's view; *"Greater love has no one than this, than to lay down one's life for his friends."*[2] How many people would you consider laying down your life for? Probably your children, your spouse, possibly other relatives, and most likely your dearest friends. They would have to be dearest friends, though. No fair-weather friends would make this list. How about an enemy? How about that crotchety neighbor you have contended with for years? Or that lying sneak of a co-worker who got himself promoted to a job rightfully yours? Would you lay down your life for the mailman, your hairdresser, the trash man, or the telephone operator? Most of us, if we would even consider giving up our life, would have very extensive criteria for qualified individuals, and you can be sure it would not include anyone who has *ever* sinned against us—no statute of limitations here.

God and His beloved Son Jesus felt a little differently about love. God gave up His only Son. Jesus died for us while we were still sinners! This is the ultimate sacrifice, this is above and beyond—*this* is love. Can you grasp the depth and breadth of this one incredible act? When you look at the cross and revisit the Calvary walk, do you understand the magnitude of love as God defines it? I don't believe it is humanly possible to fully grasp this immense love, but it *is* possible to strive toward it

> Jesus died for us while we were still sinners! This is the ultimate sacrifice, this is above and beyond—*this* is love.

and view all of our circumstances and relationships with the cross as a backdrop. Let's look at 1 Corinthians 13, piece by piece.

LOVE SUFFERS LONG AND IS KIND

Love suffers long. The crux of our being is, first, our relationship with God, then our relationship with each other. When I think of the suffering within these relationships I think about how we hurt God and each other, and that immediately brings me to the subject of forgiveness. We are called to forgive, no matter how much someone hurts us, no matter how much we suffer. We are called to seek forgiveness if we have hurt others or have caused them to suffer. Scripture says, *"And be kind to one another, tenderhearted, forgiving one another, even as God in Christ forgave you."*[3] That is a tough pill to swallow. We don't want to forgive people who cause us pain. That means we have to give up the right to hurt them the way they have hurt us. It lets them off the hook. By not forgiving, we can continue to make them suffer for their sins against us. But, it also has effects on *us* that we may fail to recognize.

When we refuse to forgive, hurt turns to bitterness and bitterness becomes cancerous. It festers within us and can manifest itself in physical and emotional ways. I saw that happen with my own mother. She had a stroke about seven years before she died. It was a very stressful time for my father and my sister and me as we tried to help him care for her. She continually berated people, told my father she hated him, and relived her hatred for people from situations long in her past. She hated her only sister, her mother, her aunt, someone who stole from her (no one knows who), and on and on it went. My father was emotionally and physically drained and I believe the cancer that later took his life was a direct result of that.

The doctors told us that our mother's mental health had deteriorated to an irreversible state. It was senseless for my dad to continue to try to reason or argue with her. Although we tried to reinforce the doctor's words we found ourselves sucked into her bantering after only a short time in her presence. Those intense seven years gave daily expression to the anger and bitterness that she harbored all of her life because she had never learned to forgive. Surely, her mother treated her badly and her sister may have been unkind to her, but what satisfaction did she gain by clinging to resentment? Who was this person she hated so fiercely who stole a small trinket from her so long ago? I don't know. But, I do know this, what was really stolen from her, because of her unwillingness to forgive, was peace and joy.

Forgiving my mother after years of abuse would have been impossible without Gods grace. He helped me see that her anger toward her mother was the result of her experience of abuse from both her parents. It helped me realize that she did the best she could under the circumstances. That understanding also helped me to accept myself as a parent who struggles with inadequacies.

The sexual abuse was probably the most difficult hurt to overcome. For years I kept that dark secret, until one day a friend began sharing her experience of abuse when she was younger. For the first time, I told my story. And together, with God, we struggled through the pain that I had long denied. Finally, I was able to forgive and that forgiveness gave me indescribable grace and peace. However, I would be remiss if I did not admit that there are parts of that experience that may never heal. But, the impact it has on my life has been greatly diminished.

Another difficult situation I had to deal with happened several years ago when I brought a friend into a business I had started. Our business was doing very well, but things were not right between us, and we did not share the same beliefs regarding treatment of employees and each other. Consequently, I made the decision to divide the business and dissolve our partnership. Afterward, she made some unethical decisions that caused me some financial loss. I felt cheated and very hurt by someone I had once considered a friend.

I had two options: I could hurt her by revealing information about her unethical practices, or I could back off. Revealing the information would have given me some satisfaction, while backing off

> Bitterness is like taking rat poison and waiting for the rat to die. Can you get a vivid picture of that?

would mean that I would have to accept things for what they were and move on. Remembering how an unwillingness to forgive had caused so much bitterness and unhappiness in my parent's lives, I chose to move on. I wrote a letter to her simply telling her that although what she did to me was wrong, I forgave her. I have never had to look back, and I have never had a moment of regret for my actions. I recently heard that bitterness is like taking rat poison and waiting for the rat to die. Can you get a vivid picture of that?

What is it that allows some people to freely forgive while others find it impossible? I believe that forgiving *is* impossible if a person is not in a relationship with God. I don't mean an occasional nod toward heaven, an envelope in the basket, or even vast knowledge of Scripture. I mean a relationship that calls us out of complacency and places us face to face with the living God. Considering a relationship with God can be as difficult as some earthly relationships. We simply don't want to get involved. We throw a coin into the lap of a beggar, but walk quickly away, not wanting to engage him. We may send a card to a neighbor who lost a loved one, but won't knock on the door to offer comfort. We'll cross the street to avoid a teen who dresses strangely, and *never, never* go near a person with AIDS. Relationships require something from us. They require honesty, commitment, trust, risk, openness, willingness to change, and, yes—sometimes giving up our desires, for the good of the other person. Relationships can be demanding, so we tend to avoid many of them. The same is true of our avoidance of God. He might ask us to do something we don't want to do. Like, oh, I don't know…*forgive* maybe?

We cannot forgive others because we see *them* as our enemy. But, it is Satan who is our enemy, not that other person. You know the scene depicted in Matthew where Jesus is telling His disciples that it is time for Him to go to Jerusalem to suffer and die? And Peter pipes up and says, *"Far be it from You, Lord; this shall not happen to you."*[4] What arrogance Peter had, to think He could rewrite Jesus' destiny. And what did Jesus say to him? Not, "get behind Me Peter, you are standing in the way of providence," but, rather, *"Get behind Me Satan! You are an offense to Me."*[5] Jesus knew Peter meant well and that he loved Him, and He knew Satan was the evil one behind Peter's words. Satan does his best work in us when we keep our distance from God. He does his best to pit us against each other in every way he can. When bitterness and hatred keep us out of relationship with God, Satan wins.

Henry and Richard Blackaby, in their book *Experiencing God*, say, "Forgiveness is not a spiritual gift, a skill, or an inherited trait. Forgiveness is a choice. Jesus looked down on those who had ruthlessly and mockingly nailed Him to a cross, yet He cried out, *"Father, forgive them, for they do not know what they do."*[6] How, then, can we refuse to forgive those who have committed offenses against us?[7]

Doing the things God calls me to do that are humanly impossible shows the sovereignty of God like nothing else can. There is a true story that depicts that truth in a powerful way. A few years ago two days before Christmas, a couple lost their only son, 18 years old, to a drunk driver. The couple had so much hatred for the young man who killed their son that they tracked his every moment, intent on revenge. The mother said, "All I can think of is that he should die and how he should die." Over time, as his case moved through the court system, the couple was there and heard the story of his life. The details of his background began to change the way they looked at him. If I told you their hearts softened and they were able to forgive that young man, would you find that amazing? If I told you they grew to love him as their own, would you find that impossible? But, would you *see* Jesus in that couple? Of course you would, and that is why God says, unequivocally, *"For if you forgive their trespasses, your heavenly Father will also forgive you. But if you do not forgive men their trespasses, neither will your Father forgive your trespasses."*[8] Why is He so stubborn on this one? Because, like everything else He expects of us, He knows this act will return indescribable gifts to us as well as to the people we forgive.

When I was a child, my brother and sister, both older than me, would tell me our parents found me under a rock; I believed them. When we are unforgiving to others aren't we, in essence, telling them the same thing? We have this pious attitude that says, "I am a child of God, but you must have been found under a rock. You are not as good as me—you are a sinner and I am not."

Because forgiving is the most difficult thing for us to do, it becomes the ultimate expression of love. Did Jesus not express that on the cross? Don't think for a moment that God doesn't know how difficult it is. God knows because He sent His only Son to His death, so that our sins might be forgiven. He didn't just forgive the other guy's sins, but He also forgave yours and mine.

When we suffer sorrow and pain at the hands of another, endure that suffering, and then show kindness towards them—we are demonstrating the unconditional love of God. There is an expression that I have never forgotten—we only love God as much as the person we hate the most. Think about that!

The other side of this coin is asking for forgiveness. Years ago, there was a movie titled, "Love Story," in which a woman (Ali McGraw) said to her husband (Ryan O'Neal), "love means never having to say you're sorry." Give me a break. That is just not right. But it feels good because we don't like to be wrong and we sure don't like others to tell us we're wrong. However, there is a profound sense of humility within a person who can ask for forgiveness.

If asking for forgiveness is a measure of humility, then I should be the poster child for it. Unfortunately, I am always having to ask for forgiveness because I am always saying something that requires it. My brain processes while my mouth is engaged, that is a prescription for trouble. Usually, the process of rectifying the situation brings a lesson for me that I am thankful for. However, there are times when a plea for forgiveness falls on deaf ears and I have to accept that. We are called to rectify the wrongs we do, but we are not responsible for the response of the other person. Yes, love does mean saying your sorry, and it means forgiving others—even if they aren't sorry.

LOVE DOES NOT ENVY

Ouch. Do you have a friend who has just met the man of her dreams, and you are looking at that lump on the sofa who is guzzling beer and belching show tunes while you wonder where you went wrong? Shame on you. Are you wearing the outside garments of humility while your undergarments are bunched up because your neighbor just bought a new car? Your lacy envy is showing. Why is it so hard for us to be content? A recent study showed the average American will spend 9 years of his or her life in front of a TV. I wonder how many years of our lives are wasted on envy or trying to accumulate *things* to one-up our neighbors.

Most of my life I have spent being envious of someone— if not a relative or neighbor, then a character on TV. Someone was always prettier, wealthier, or thinner. Her house was bigger, her kids were better-behaved, her husband was more loving, her dog could talk—okay, maybe the dog couldn't talk. The great paradox here is that envy will usually give way to pride. "Well, if I can't *really* be better, then I will just pretend I am." How much we are hurting God, like a spoiled child always wanting more, "That's not fair! How come she got more than me?!" Envy leaves a hole in our hearts that cannot be filled and it prevents us from receiving the fullness of God's blessings.

I now look for people to admire. My hero is Mother Teresa. The example of her life, lived simply, convicts me of the sinfulness and unholiness of Envy and Envy's evil twin, Pride. Mother Teresa lived what she taught, a life of poverty equal to the poor she served. She could have lived in the lap of luxury. Benefactors were continually trying to lavish her with material possessions, only to find them sold and the money used for the poor. How much room would be left in your closet if Mother Teresa's only two changes of clothes were hung there? Well, actually one—the other she wore.

God admonishes us for our envious ways, *"Who is wise and understanding among you? Let him show by good conduct that his works are done in the meekness of wisdom. But if you have bitter envy and self-seeking in your hearts, do not boast and lie against the truth. This wisdom does not descend from above, but is earthly, sensual, and demonic. For where envy and self-seeking exist, confusion and every evil thing are there."*[9]

> Jesus got what He didn't deserve, for sinners—undeserving. Will your longing wane; will your envy seem trite? It should.

I have another hero. He was born in poverty, lived in poverty, and died in poverty. His name is Jesus. The next time you feel a twinge of envy, of desire for that which you think you deserve, I pray you will get a picture of Calvary. Jesus got what He didn't deserve, for sinners—undeserving. Will your longing wane; will your envy seem trite? It should. Love sends envy an eviction notice and fills it's space with gratitude.

DOES NOT GET PUFFED UP

"Everyone proud in heart is an abomination to the Lord."[10] An abomination is an object of hatred. God HATES pride. Does that adequately describe God's antipathy toward the arrogance and self-righteousness that are manifested from a prideful heart? Slithering under the rock of every evil imaginable is that maggot, Pride. That's why God hates it and Satan loves it. How difficult is it to eradicate pride from our lives? Ask Jesus' disciples who competed for a favored spot next to Him; they deserved it didn't they?

How about that Nebuchadnezzar? *"The king spoke saying, 'Is not this great Babylon, that I have built for a royal dwelling by my mighty power and for the honor of my majesty."*[11] Well, *la-de-hoop-de-do-da,* aren't you a piece of work. And didn't your Mighty God notice your mighty arrogance? Buddy, you are in big trouble. While the ole' boys words were still in his mouth, God's response was swift and just, He took away his kingdom and sent him packing. "Go live like the beasts of the field. You're gonna smell funny and look funny when this is all over and then we'll talk about your attitude problem." God said, *"... They shall make you eat grass like oxen; and seven times shall pass over you, until you know that the Most High rules in the kingdom of men, and gives it to whomever He chooses."*[12] There, take that you fool! Do you suppose he learned his lesson? You bet he did, *"I lifted my eyes to heaven, and my understanding returned to me; and I blessed the Most High and praised and honored Him who lives forever."*[13]

Do you suppose Jonah learned his lesson after the whale regurgitated his sorry self? At first glance it appears he finally saw the light! God told him, "Pick yourself up and go straight to Nineveh and preach My message. Oh and Jonah, you might want to clean up a little first. Whew!" Jonah obeyed. No questions asked. But, he was hoping God's message would fall on deaf ears and the people there would feel God's wrath. No doubt his imagination was going wild with thoughts of how God would deal with them.

Soon Jonah got to the city and shouted, *"Yet forty days, and Nineveh shall be overthrown!"*[14] Can you hear it in his voice? That snicker? That sense of sweet revenge? "Now, you're gonna get it!" But to his amazement and embarrassment, this entire heathen city dropped to their knees and began to praise God. When God saw their collective change of heart, He relented and spared them. When Jonah saw that, he was fit to be tied. He just couldn't get beyond his prideful heart.

Raise your hand if you know someone who exudes a prideful attitude; raise your hand if pride is not an issue for you; raise your hand if you're lying! If you're not sure, I can help; I have a lot of experience in pointing out other's faults. My prayer could have been, *"God, I thank thee, that I am not as other men are…"*[15]

Now I stand with the tax collector, the prostitute, and anyone else who shouts from the depths of their soul, "I am not worthy, I am a sinner; I cannot save myself." AHA! That's it—that is the ultimate truth about the ultimate sin. Pride says, I can take care of myself, I don't need God; humility says I am nothing without God. Jesus said it too, *"I can of Myself do nothing."*[16] Did you hear that? Can you fathom the perfect Jesus, God's beloved Son, acknowledging His total dependence on His Father?

> Each time my ego clouds my vision I am reminded: while I am puffed up, Jesus is slumped over—on the cross, for me.

We are a nation bent on independence and self-sufficiency. Humility is the round peg in the square hole of self-righteousness. It has taken me a long time to pray for humility. It is said to be careful of what you pray for. God may have a lesson in pride for me that I won't be crazy about. Although I am a vegetarian, I am not particularly fond of grass! (You know, that whole Nebuchadnezzar thing? I thought I lost you for a minute). Each time my ego clouds my vision I am reminded: while I am puffed up, Jesus is slumped over—on the cross, for me.

DOES NOT BEHAVE RUDELY; IS NOT PROVOKED

The word rude doesn't sound that bad, really. It sounds like a slight burp in public: "Oh, excuse me, it slipped." Webster begs to differ. The reality of rude is a lot harsher: "uncivilized, violent." We're not talking about a little rudeness here; we're talking about out-and-out anger.

Is all anger wrong? God got angry, really angry, and didn't mince words when He did. In many verses throughout Scripture, He admonished His people, calling them liars, adulterers, idolaters, and self-righteous fools. He speaks to Judah, *"You have kindled a fire in My anger which shall burn forever!"*[17] Do you detect a little anger here? Stick with me because this could seem contradictory at first glance. Is that God being angry? But, doesn't He tell us anger is bad? Is this don't do as I do, do as I say? If you want to see real anger played out in stereo, read the Book of Jeremiah. It's in there, all the anger, hurt, and pain known to man. Chapter 25 is really scary. *"The Lord will roar from on high,*[18] *...they shall become refuse on the ground,*[19] *Wail, shepherds, and cry! Roll about in the ashes, you leaders of the flock! For the days of your slaughter and your dispersions are fulfilled...because of the fierce anger of the Lord."*[20] It doesn't start there and it doesn't end there. God lamented the sins of His children, and in particular the leaders, all throughout this book.

So, when my husband provokes me to anger, it's okay to vent? When my son wrecks the car, it is acceptable to rage after him if I can't control myself? No, and that's where we need to recognize the difference. God was expressing righteous anger. His people continued to turn their backs on Him and sin was ramped. His judgment was harshest on the leaders. They were responsible for the care of His people, instead they lead His people astray and turned them away from God. God knew their continued sin would be the ruin of mankind. Man's sinfulness forced His hand.

Anger can also surface in the act of vengeance. That too is unacceptable. Remember, God has told us since the beginning of time it is His alone to right the wrongs of others who harm us. He says, "*Beloved, do not avenge yourselves, but rather give place to wrath; for it is written, 'Vengeance is Mine, I will repay.'* "[21]

So, how can we recognize unrighteous anger? When it gives voice to unmet needs. I have lived with anger all my life and have myself, since childhood, cowered behind it when the bullies in my life have accosted me—the parent bully, the teacher bully, the husband bully, the child bully, the checker at the grocery store bully, the whoever-crosses-my-PMS-path bully. I always excused my actions as victim status justification. But there is no justification for lashing out at someone, for firing those poison darts of angry words that embed themselves into the hearts of others.

As a child my outbursts came in the form of slamming doors and mumbles of "I hate you!" under my breath. Because I withdrew more and more I took on a sense of feeling invisible. The longing I had to be recognized was fertile soil for the festering anger that was growing inside of me. As I grew older and knew I was no longer under the "control" of someone bigger than me, I gave myself the freedom to express that anger without fear of parental punishment. Each outburst revealed a child within screaming, "Pay attention to me!" There was no room for sensitivity to others' feelings; I was too busy protecting my own.

My husband also came into our relationship with plenty of baggage. So, between the two of us clamoring for attention, our relationship was volatile from the beginning. I will never forget the day we were at his mother's house before the wedding. We were paying for the wedding ourselves so we had to cut costs as much as possible. I decided to make my own invitations, and we were working on them when, for whatever reason, Tom and I began screaming at each other. We carried it outside, as my intent was to walk home. Inside, his mother sat in front of the typewriter wondering if she should continue. Both of our families understandably questioned, some more vocally than others, whether we were making the right decision. At the very least we should have recognized an ensuing problem and gotten help. Unfortunately, premarital counseling was non-existent for us. Thus began many years of battles that not only damaged our lives, but our children's as well.

I have been able to come to the realization that other people are just as broken as I am, and they are incapable of meeting my needs. That realization coupled with the understanding that God, and only God, can meet those needs, has brought me great peace. Am I perfect? No, and I do still struggle and find myself striking out at times. The difference is that it isn't as frequent, the words aren't as stinging, and apologies come more swiftly.

Anger can, at times, be justified. But, there is a fine line between justified and unjustified anger. Healthy anger can motivate people to accomplish or change things. Unhealthy anger strikes out and hurts others. How often do we hear or say to ourselves, "I can't help myself, it's just the way I am." Not so, says Neil Clark Warren, "Important findings from psychological research indicate that how you choose to use your anger is learned. And you can bring it under the control of your thinking and decision making."[22] Learning that difficult but powerful lesson has allowed me to go to everyone I have hurt in anger and ask for forgiveness. It has had tremendous healing power for me. Unfortunately, those we hurt are sometimes not able to forgive us and are left with scars that may never heal. We need to quit playing the blame game and take responsibility for our actions. God wants to help and He can heal.

This was the area of my life where my greatest failures were birthed, this wild-eyed creature of Satan's joy. But, it was also the springboard to my relationship with God. It was out of the depths of my longing to change that I turned to Scripture in search of answers and found a merciful, loving God. Scripture tells us Mary Magdalene, Mary the mother of James, and Salome headed to Jesus' tomb with spices to anoint Him and were greeted with the shock of their lives. Jesus was gone! A young man in a long white robe, standing in the tomb, shows them He is not there and tells them, *"But go, tell His disciples—and Peter...."*[23] Do you see that? Go, tell His disciples—and Peter. Peter "the rock,"...yeah, when times were swell, that is. But, when the kitchen heated up, Peter headed out. Imagine if you can, those days following Jesus' death. Peter was devastated, he "wept bitterly." He blew it big time and was sure he would never have another chance. How could he face people, how could he go on, what would he do? "Go tell His disciples— and Peter." Make sure you tell Peter and make sure you tell Linda. God wants them to know how much He loves them— in spite of their sins.

> *This was the area of my life where my greatest failures were birthed... But, it was also the springboard to my relationship with God.*

"LOVE THINKS NO EVIL; DOES NOT REJOICE IN INIQUITY, BUT REJOICES IN THE TRUTH"

I have to make a confession here. When I heard that Martha Stewart was in trouble because of the possibility of unethical trading practices, a smile swept across my face. Not nice. Sorry, I lost my head.

But, could we not find lots of people today to hate or to wish evil upon? Just pick up the paper: the list grows daily of executives who skim millions of dollars from their company coffers, pad the books, and mislead investors and employees, for their own personal gain. Their indiscretions and greed are almost beyond comprehension.

Most of us don't need to look that far to find people who make messes in our lives. Isn't there something we should do to make them pay? The answer is a simple and emphatic, NO! God will take care of it and we are not to worry about it. He says, *"Do not fret because of evildoers, nor be envious of the workers of iniquity. For they shall soon be cut down like the grass, and wither as the green herb."*24 No snickering allowed here; we are not to wish evil on anyone.

If we do things God's way, we will experience God's victory. The truth is, God hates a pious attitude that wishes for evil to repay evil. We need to let go of things that we have no control over and live as God calls us to. And what does He call us to do when we want to get the voodoo doll and the pins out? He wants us to pray instead. That's right, we are to pray for our enemies and for their salvation, *"Do not rejoice when your enemy falls, and do not let your heart be glad when he stumbles; lest the Lord see it, and it displeases Him, and he turn away His wrath from him."*25 If you wish for evil and rejoice when it comes, what is the glory in that? If you pray for those who hurt you, can you see the glory in that? That person may just come to know God because of your efforts. The angels rejoice and heaven sings when one lost soul is found.

BEARS ALL THINGS; BELIEVES ALL THINGS; HOPES ALL THINGS; ENDURES ALL THINGS

When your husband comes home drunk, again; when your child is arrested on drug charges; when your cancer has returned; when your aging parents make continual demands; when your electric has been shut off and your car breaks down on the highway; when you can't lift your head off the pillow to face another day—how do you bear up, believe, hope, endure? You cry out to God in despair and you don't get an answer. How do you go on? You have to believe in your heart that the God of mercy, the God who gave up His only Son for you, loves you immeasurably more than you can imagine. Nothing you grieve is without a purpose, nor does it go unheard.

In the book of Genesis, Abraham was called by God to slay his beloved son, Isaac. Could I have trusted God that much? There was no secret spy in this story, "psssssssst, Abe, just go along with it, He'll stop you at the last minute, trust me." Abraham completely trusted God—I can't say I would do the same. The Lord's most beloved disciples were martyred for their faithfulness and trust in God.

Paul continually calls us to faithfulness and courage, *"Do you not know that those who run in a race all run, but one receives the prize? Run in such a way that you may obtain it."*[26] *"Watch, stand fast in faith, be brave, be strong. Let all that you do be done with love."*[27] And then, *"Blessed be the God and Father of our Lord Jesus Christ, the Father of mercies and God of all comfort, who comforts us in all our tribulations, that we may be able to comfort those who are in any trouble, with the comfort with which we ourselves are comforted by God."*[28] 2 Corinthians says, *"We are hard-pressed on every side, yet not crushed; we are perplexed, but not in despair; persecuted, but not forsaken; struck down, but not destroyed…"*[29] Paul was persecuted, jailed, abandoned, and martyred and yet he gave thanks and praise to God. *"I now rejoice in my sufferings for you…"*[30] He was given a "thorn in his flesh" and pleaded with God three times to remove it, *"and He said to me, 'My grace is sufficient for you, for My strength is made perfect in weakness.' Therefore I take pleasure in infirmities, in reproaches, in needs, in persecutions, in distresses, for Christ's sake. For when I am weak, then I am strong."*[31]

We can find incredible stories up to the present of people who have suffered.

There are countless stories of survivors of concentration camps during World War II. David Pelzer, in his incredible book, *A Child Called "It,"*[32] tells his story of abuse that was one of the worst cases of child abuse ever recorded in California. There are thousands of examples of people who survived the unthinkable. How? By knowing and believing in God's promises. Through the darkness of despair comes the dawn of grace. When you can't see or hear Him in the midst of your pain, trust His heart of love for you at the core of your being. *"Blessed are those who suffer well and hope for things unseen, for theirs is the kingdom of God"* (Matthew 5). Our suffering has a higher purpose—in suffering we learn to comfort others.

I was a youth minister for nine years, working with high school kids in my church. I loved the teens and I believe the heart I had for them grew from my own struggles growing up. I encountered several kids who's obnoxious behavior would send most adults running for cover. Not me. I tried to look beyond the behavior, to the inside. I felt the behavior was usually a manifestation of something deeper.

A great example was a boy, I'll call him Joe, who came to youth group with his brother. He would come faithfully every week and sit on the fringe of every discussion and activity his arms tightly wrapped around himself, as a means of protection from the world around him. For the life of me, I didn't understand why he came week after week. He was negative about everything we did. Engaging him in our discussions was always a challenge. Except for admonishing any negative behavior, I did my best to accept him where he was and the other kids did as well.

I discovered a little about his background. It seemed his parents had sent both boys to a very exclusive, private grade school with a challenging curriculum. His brother thrived—Joe did not. Joe's parents and his brother continually berated him because he was not as smart and didn't try hard enough.

My challenge was to encourage him and find ways to show him his worth. I would pray for God to give me opportunities to do that—He did. We were sitting in a circle discussing an issue and as usual Joe had his chair pushed back outside the circle. One of the questions they were asked to consider had two possible answers. Everyone's response was the same, except Joe's. I looked at him and said, "Well, that's interesting. How did you come to that conclusion?" He explained, and I was amazed because his reason was really valid. I then said to him, "Wow, that's awesome. I would never have thought of that." The other kids, with the exception of his brother, affirmed him as well. Suddenly, he looked at his brother and said, "See, I'm not so dumb after all." And with that, he scooted his chair into the circle! The change in him from that day forward was a testimony to what I have continually believed about people. We struggle and we hurt, but God uses it for good, *"But as for you, you meant evil against me; but God meant it for good, in order to bring it about as it is this day, to save many people alive."*[33]

What if Jesus' story had been different? What if He would have gone to the cross kicking and screaming? He had a right. He was being persecuted unfairly. In His lifetime He had done nothing but love His Father and mankind, for that He was beaten. He could have retaliated with an army of angels, but He kept them silent. He healed the sick, brought hope to the hopeless, and forgave the sinner. For that He was stripped, spit on, and mocked. He could have cursed them to Hell and His Father could have arranged the trip, but God quietly wept for the love of His only Son.

For all the love Jesus gave the world, the world returned hatred in the form of a cross. The nails did not hold Him there, His love held Him there. His last words could have been shouts of angry vengeance. He had the power to make it happen, but He chose to forgive in that final act of mercy. Why? He caused the Roman soldier to proclaim, *"Truly this*

man was the Son of God!"[34] Peter said, *"For Christ also suffered once for sins, the just for the unjust, that He might bring
us to God..."*[35] That's why, and that is why He calls us to do
the same. As for your trials, *"...rejoice to the extent that you
partake of Christ's sufferings, that when His glory is revealed,
you may also be glad with exceeding joy. If you are reproached
for the name of Christ, blessed are you, for the Spirit of glory
and of God rests upon you. On their part He is blasphemed,
but on your part He is glorified. Yet if anyone suffers as a
Christian, let him not be ashamed, but let him glorify God in
this matter."*[36]

    I will let my mother-in-law show you why God calls us to
bear all things, hope all things, believe all things, endure all
things. Twenty-nine years ago I stood before her in short
skirts and long wigs. I had a seven-year-old daughter, and a
heathen attitude. I was self-centered and demanding and
resented the frequent times my husband would call and tell
me he was stopping to see her after work. I would be angry
that he spent so much time with her. I was jealous. She could
have done what everyone else in my life had done: rejected
me or struck out at me. I could have understood that reaction, it was what I was use to. Instead, she chose to love me,
in spite of myself, and soon I was drawn to her. She had
something I wanted, and I didn't even know what it was.
After being in her company and experiencing first hand her
selfless love for others, and me, I was hooked.

    She brought me to the throne of God where I began the
long journey of change. Today, at 85, she is still giving of herself. She has born the pain of losing a younger sister to cancer,
as well as a beloved son, and struggled through a difficult marriage. Yet, she has continued to reach out and love others. She
has endured much for One, Jesus. If it were not for witnessing
her faith and hope in the midst of suffering, I would most
likely still be wearing those dreaded short skirts, still be self-
absorbed, and would have missed the blessings God has

> C. S. Lewis said about love, "The only place outside Heaven where you can be perfectly safe from all the dangers and perturbations of love is Hell."

poured on me. There are many other lost Lindas out there—have you touched one lately? Or have you turned one away?

THE GREATEST OF THESE IS LOVE

C. S. Lewis said about love, "The only place outside Heaven where you can be perfectly safe from all the dangers and perturbations of love is Hell."[37]

Scripture tells us the value God places on love, *"And now abide faith, hope, love, these three; but the greatest of these is love."*[38] The *greatest* of these is love. Love is a verb; it's an action word. It is not enough to give it lip service and assume we are fulfilling God's commandment to love one another. If the actions don't match the words, they are a lie; whether we are talking about our love for God or our neighbor. When Jesus died on the cross He went beyond *telling* us He loved us, He *showed* us—and He commands us to do the same. 1 John tells all about how and why to love the people in our lives, *"If someone says, 'I love God,' and hates his brother, he is a liar; for he who does not love his brother whom he has seen, how can he love God whom he has not seen?"*[39] I'm sure we could all point a finger at someone like that, but is someone pointing their finger back at us? *"My little children, let us not love in word or in tongue, but in deed and in truth."*[40]

Chapter Two

JOY

"Shout joyfully to the Lord, all the earth;
break forth in song, rejoice, and sing praises."[1]

All right, let's do just that. I have the perfect song. If you don't know this one just hum along with us. Ready?

I've got the joy, joy, joy, joy, down in my heart—hey!

down in my heart—whoa!

down in my heart—yeah!

I've got the joy, joy, joy, joy, down in my heart, down in my heart to stay!!

From the back of the crowd certain rumblings can be heard: "Oh, puhleeezeee! Give me a break!"

"Excuse me?"

"You heard me. I suppose you just hit the lottery, is that it? Maybe you tried that new miracle diet pill and really did wake up this morning twenty pounds lighter. What is it? Why are you making me want to slap you into seriousness? If you had my life you would have nothing to sing about. My husband left me for a younger woman and I was just laid-off my job. Maybe your life is perfect, but mine is falling apart. So—hum that one for me!"

Well, okay. We'll forget the song for now, but not the joy. Just stay with me here a minute.

JOY ESCAPED ME

I am a convert—from an indifferent, self-absorbed life, to a Christian. Or what I prefer—a disciple. But it has not been a smooth journey. I spent most of the last twenty-five years in the process, taking the proverbial one step forward and six steps back. Those few steps forward would be lost to the backsliding of selfish demands: "Fix him, fix her, and I will take another step. Give me more, make the pain go away, and I will try again. This is too hard Lord. I expected when You washed away my sins that somehow You would wash away all the heartache too. What's the point if the suffering is the same?"

> Cynicism is the devil's tool to keep unbelievers away from salvations door.

JOY ESCAPES MOST PEOPLE

This world seems to be going to Hell in a hand-basket and it seems unstoppable.

"So why shouldn't we be cynical? Come on, we're waiting."

Since you asked, I'll tell you—because cynicism is the devil's tool to keep unbelievers away from salvations door.

"Look," says the non-believer, "they're just as miserable as we are, maybe more so, because they have all those 'thou shalt not's' to live with. If I'm going to be miserable I might as well do it on my own terms."

Joy Never Escaped Jesus

No one suffered as much as Jesus did: the loss of His friends, the beatings, the cruel mockery, and the final horrible death. That is a sobering truth that would steal anyone's joy. I am as sorrowful as the next person every time I contemplate the Crucifixion. The pain Jesus suffered was beyond our human comprehension. We need to be reminded of that when we wander away from God. But is it Jesus' death that brought us to the foot of the cross to begin with? I submit to you, on the contrary, that it is the resurrection that brings us to Him and compels us to follow Him. And He knew that at the Last Supper. He told His disciples, *"These things I have spoken to you that My joy may remain in you, and that your joy may be complete."*[2] Do you see that? Where does He say, "Boy this stinks, wipe those smiles off your faces! I want you to be miserable and mourn for Me the rest of your natural lives?" Who wants to hang out with a miserable, joyless person? Jesus had to encourage His disciples because they were heading down that path of despair. They were confused and terrified. He told them, *"Most assuredly, I say to you that you will weep and lament, but the world will rejoice; and you will be sorrowful, but your sorrow will be turned into joy."*[3]

He was going to give them their time to grieve. But in order for them to fulfill His command to go and bear fruit, they would have to change that sorrow to joy—if they were going to succeed in bringing people to Christ.

That is a message that seems to have been lost to Jonah. The *last* thing he wanted was to bring the Ninevites to God. He longed for them to crash and burn. Over the years, I have heard his message—not the *Good News* message, but the "you're going to burn in hell if you don't change your ways" message, from many so-called Christians. And I can assure you, it only served to fan the flames of Satan's stronghold on me.

JESUS FILLED HIS DISCIPLES WITH JOY

Let's revisit that scene in the upper room. You know, where the disciples are bemoaning their situation and their state of unemployment. Peter probably decides he'll go back to fishing. "Three years training out the window, woe is me." Matthew contemplates going back to school. Thomas decides to take some vacation time. Some of the others chime in, in agreement. Suddenly, Jesus is in their midst. He only has a short layover. No time to waste. He gives them clear understanding, softens their hearts, and gives them their marching orders. This rag-tag bunch of whiners and complainers are transformed into mighty warriors for the Kingdom. They are a-hootin' and a-hollarin' and chompin at the bit to share in the suffering of Christ. Were they crazy?

Jesus told them they would be rejected, persecuted, run out of town, stoned, and beheaded. Volunteers stepped forward. In unison they stepped forward and never looked back. The cock could crow 'til the sun went down and none of them would falter, none would turn tail and run. Not this time.

Scripture is replete with Peter and Paul's letters that describe their "happy trails" to martyrdom. They continually encouraged their followers to have the same courage and joy for Christ. They were resistant to all attempts to subvert their allegiance to God. Each time Paul went to jail, he went singing and praising God. You think I'm making this up don't you? Well, I encourage you to read Philippians, or 1 and 2 Peter, or 1, 2, and 3 John, and much of everything in-between. Start anywhere, close your eyes and point randomly to a verse, you're going to find "joy" everywhere you look. Let me show you just a few examples:

"But at midnight Paul and Silas were praying and singing hymns to God, and the prisoners were listening to them."[4] You'll

notice the prisoners weren't saying, "Hey, will you guys knock it off! We're trying to sleep here!" On the contrary, they were taking copious notes. And when that whole earthquake thing happened and their shackles fell to the floor, they dropped to their knees to praise God in the same way they saw Paul and Silas praising Him earlier.

Paul tells them, *"But I want you to know, brethren, that the things which happened to me have actually turned out for the furtherance of the gospel, so that it has become evident to the whole palace guard, and to all the rest, that my chains are in Christ; and most of the brethren in the Lord, having become confident by my chains, are much more bold to speak the word without fear."*[5]

Again he says, *"…according to my earnest expectation and hope that in nothing I shall be ashamed, but with all boldness, as always, so now also Christ will be magnified in my body."*[6]

He calls his followers to do the same, *"Do all things without complaining and disputing, that you may become blameless and harmless, children of God without fault in the midst of a crooked and perverse generation, among whom you shine as lights in the world."*[7]

"rejoice with joy inexpressible and full of glory."

Peter, too, expressed profound joy during his trials, that he was privileged to follow in Jesus' footsteps. He too, called others to not just persevere, but do it joyfully, *"In this you greatly rejoice, though not for a little while, if need be, you have been grieved by various trials, that the genuineness of your faith, being much more precious than gold that perishes, though it is tested by fire, may be found to praise, honor, and glory at the revelation of Jesus Christ…rejoice with joy inexpressible and full of glory."*[8] Joy inexpressible. WOW! That's not a simple encouragement to keep a stiff upper lip—grin and bear it. No, that is a promise of something unimaginable by the world's standards.

"*The genuineness of your faith.*" That is what Christ called His disciples to—genuineness. We all know people who spew religion from their mouths and walk stone-faced through life. You can spot them a mile away. You know the guy lurking in the shadows of a darkened storefront, wearing a long trench coat and sunglasses.

"Psssst, hey you."

"Who me?"

"Yeah you. Come here."

You hesitate. He opens his trench coat to reveal a myriad of gadgets guaranteed to get you into heaven—and a small watch collection. What are these gadgets? They are the things a good Christian can't live without: a rule book, a pitty pot, lemon juice (just in case you can't stay serious enough), a ten volume video library containing an exhaustive history of the evil in the world to keep you depressed (lest you forget); a refrigerator magnet with the fourteen Commandments, the last four are penciled in—thou shalt not smile, dance, sing, or keep company with people who do. Before you reach for your wallet, check out the trench coat. Do you see it? That little red tail sticking out from under it? Satan would love for you to buy into this lie.

Oh, you may get to heaven if you live a somber, secluded life, but you sure won't be taking anyone with you. You may have proclaimed your belief in God and His Son, Jesus Christ. But what will it look like when you stand before Him?

The last instructions Jesus gave His disciples before He departed were, "*Go, therefore, and make disciples of all the nations.*"[9] They could have sold people a bill of goods and promoted Christianity as trouble-free, but they never did. What has drawn people to Christianity down through the ages is a life that only God can offer: peace, contentment, and joy in the midst of trials.

JOY AT WHAT COST?

Oh Boy. Ohhh…Boy!! What have I done? I see what you're thinking. You're going to set the alarm. Rise at 5:00 A.M., tiptoe out of the bedroom, down the hall, pour your coffee into one of those two-quart thermoses, and jump into the car before sunrise. You're on a mission. You're going to hit every garage sale, every flea market, and every antique store in a 100-mile radius. You're going to find that torture rack, or bed-of-nails, set it up in your basement, and then…finally, you will discover the joy you have longed for. The joy that has evaded you for so long. Okay, that's enough. Turn off the ignition, open the door, and back slowly away from the car. Come on—think!

What is the likelihood that you will be called to lead a martyr's life? I'm guessing, pretty slim. And in the off chance that it would happen, I can assure you, God would have already prepared you. But, you don't have to go in search of pain and suffering to gain real joy. It is not reserved for those elite few. God longs for all of us to know great joy. Scripture says, *"The thief does not come except to steal, and to kill, and to destroy. I have come that they may have life, and that they may have it more abundantly."*[10] Isn't it great to know that we don't have to end up with our heads in a guillotine or be chained to a wall in a dungeon next to some furry guy who hasn't bathed in six months, just to experience real joy?

Isn't it wonderful that we can live a joy-filled life with relatively little effort? Wait a minute—I didn't say *that*. As a matter of fact, getting there requires a lot of work and I believe that is why so many people give up trying. It reminds me of the parable of the rich young ruler in Luke.[11] I'd like to paraphrase it.

LET'S MAKE A DEAL

This rich guy asked Jesus what he would have to do to enter the kingdom of heaven. Jesus said he should obey the commandments. The rich guy ran the list through his head.

"You mean like not committing adultery, not stealing, not bearing false witness, loving my neighbor, honoring my father and mother?" He named every one and cheerfully announced his faithfulness to all of them. "Great, yes, I do all those things. Is that it? I'm there. What a relief. That was easy—anything else?"

"Well, yes," Jesus said. "There's just one more thing."

This fellow is feeling pretty sure of himself and replies in confidence. "Sure, anything."

Jesus tells him to sell everything he has and give it to the poor and he will have treasure in heaven.

"You're kidding, right? Right?" In an all too familiar scene, Jesus shook His head, "No, I'm not kidding." So, the rich young ruler threw up his hands and walked away sad.

But it wasn't a sadness that Jesus was turning *him* away; that the kingdom was not open to him. It was a sadness that he couldn't bargain for a spot in heaven. Maybe he could have tried to dicker with Jesus "How about if I sell one house and one car, and let's see…maybe one country club membership? No? Okay. Okay, how about a house, a condo, the satellite dish, and one of my wife's minks? No? Well then, I give up; you are too hard to deal with. Let me know if you change your mind." And away he goes not realizing what he has walked away from—or maybe not even caring. It was just too high a price to pay for something he couldn't even see ahead of time. After all, he never bought anything sight unseen. Why should this be any different? This was huge. Something that would cost him everything he owned and he couldn't even see so much as a picture of it? How crazy is that?

MY DESPERATE SEARCH

When it comes to joy, Jesus is asking us to do the same thing He asked the rich young ruler. To give up our worldly pursuits, the things we treasure most, and follow Him. That is how we will find true joy. Most of my life I was not willing to do that and most of my life I was sad and honestly didn't know why. As I reflect back on those years, I see the progression to the joy I now experience. It has been gradual, probably too gradual from God's perspective. Sometimes so gradual as to not even be noticed. All the years I out-and-out rejected God, there was nothing that remotely resembled joy.

Growing up, I only recall the fighting and anger within my family. It was simply an existence. I married my first husband at the age of 17, hoping I would find happiness in that relationship. But, I discovered right from the outset that this was not going to be. He had affairs from the time we married to the time we divorced. He drank heavily and was too self-absorbed and too broken to meet my needs. So, I did the only logical thing (that's what we always think anyway). I had a baby, a beautiful daughter, named Wendy. It was now her turn to step up to the plate and fill my needs. She did a lousy job. She had nerve coming into the world with needs bigger than mine—how selfish can one be?

My unhappiness and frustration, and the revelation of several affairs, lead to a divorce. My daughter and I were then forced to move back home with my parents. I had come full circle. Now, my daughter would soon join me in the scramble for significance. What a terrible disservice we do to our loved ones transferring our own impossible demands onto them.

I became the self-absorbed one and regrettably abandoned my responsibilities as a mother in a frantic attempt to find that ever-elusive happiness. This time I searched under the rock of fleeting relationships and the bottomless glass of alcohol. I was suffering, and my precious daughter was suffering, and for what? I decided I would never know happiness. It was a word I'm not sure I could even define. I had made the decision that life was too hard and I was too tired to keep trying. So, I went to a party, drank until I could barely stand up, and got behind the wheel of my car, knowing I would crash somewhere and the pain would end. I drove as fast as that little MG would go. But, the end of that road was not the end of my story. I pulled up in my driveway, sat there, and amused myself with a litany of my stupidity. Not the least of which, was the fact that I was even lousy at killing myself.

About five years after my divorce, Tom and I were married, and had three sons in very short order. That was the beginning of my walk with God. Actually, it was more like a crawl. I had finally fallen on my knees before God and accepted Jesus as my Savior, which meant my wretched soul was saved. But was it really? I didn't look any different, I didn't feel any different, and most importantly, I didn't act any different. I was still unhappy and demanding.

Since I was a person who liked variety in my addictions, I added material possessions to my list of needs. Things—I had to have things to make me happy: clothes, a new house, a pool—blah, blah, blah. It was all about me. So, why wasn't I happy? I went to church every Sunday. I volunteered for various things. I was a youth minister for nine years. I was pretty good about praying. "Why?" I complained to God on a regular basis! Where was this happiness?

Tom and I were two broken people, but I could only see *him* as broken and needing fixing. There was nothing wrong with me—a saint in the midst of heathens! If my husband and I struggled, it was his fault. If my kids and I struggled, it was their fault. If a friend and I struggled, it was her fault. And if God and I struggled, I was sure it was because He wasn't cooperating.

JESUS' GENTLE TOUCH

As I gradually began to listen to God and His Word, He brought people alongside of me who were faithful Christians, my heart began to soften, and there became a different kind of longing. For a long time, I was not sure what it was for, I just knew it was not for anything I recognized. I was getting better at reaching out to others, and bolder at proclaiming my faith. But there was no difference in my belief that I was unworthy of anyone's love, especially God's. I could minister to others, but never allowed anyone to minister to me.

Also during this time, I was learning to become a better parent, thanks to Dr. James Dobson and Focus On The Family. Parenting skills are supposed to be passed down from generation to generation. At least, that was God's plan. But, for some people, like myself, that didn't happen. And as much as I hated the abuse I took from my own mother, and as much as I was determined to be different—I wasn't. I couldn't be, because I didn't know how. That is where Dr. Dobson came along, and I am forever grateful. I poured more and more of myself into my kids. But, as I was watching them grow up so quickly, a reality was setting in; Tom and I were headed for disaster and I knew it. I would beg him to look honestly at our relationship and prayed we could work harder to mend the past hurts, and work to strengthen our marriage. My pleading fell on deaf ears and my fears would soon become a reality. One by one, our children left home and left a huge hole in my heart. We were lost in the deafening silence of our "empty nest." After much thought, counseling, and prayer, I finally made the heart-wrenching decision to leave. We had to do the most difficult thing ever in our married lives—tell the kids. They all reacted differently, but one thing is true, no matter what your child's age, the separation of parents is devastating. Don't ever tell yourself anything different.

I decided to go to Kentucky for a year to volunteer for an organization that worked with the poor in Appalachia. Before I left, I prayed a prayer to God that I had never prayed before. (You know that expression to watch what you pray for? Well, it's true!) I prayed that God would change me. Not every other person in my life, *Me*! I imagine God had to get confirmation from the Holy Spirit, "Did she say what I think she said? Alright!" Well, my friends, I could write a book about the lessons God taught me while I was there. (Oh, wait—this is a book)

First, we had to get straight who the boss was. I was thinking it was me. Boy, was I wrong! I went to Kentucky for an interview to determine where I would be working. I had planned to work in Mount Vernon, which was only seven hours from home, and I planned to work with teenagers, because that's where my experience was. From prior experience I refused to work with four-year-olds. (Pre-school teachers—you are saints.) I was asked to work at the teen center in Louisa, which was another two hours away, but I accepted. It turned out to be an awful experience. I struggled and struggled in relationship with the people who ran the program. The director informed me that there would be changes and asked if I would consider staying. I declined, due to the fact that my relationship with the teens had been compromised because of things that had been said to them about me. She understood and we discussed my options. I began to pray that God would reveal His will in this decision, and I added my desire to move to Mount Vernon. The next day, I received a phone call from my director. She said there was an opening in Mount Vernon. YEAH!. I was to report to the Head Start Center on Monday morning. UGH!. A center for four-year-olds. Twenty-two to be exact.

All right, so the boss thing was settled and God's work could begin—and begin it did. There is not enough time or paper to relate to you all the cleaning out of my soul He did during the first seven months I was there. Now, you have to get this picture, okay? You've been to the mall and seen a dad, say he's about six foot tall; he's walking a little guy, just toddling. Dad is walking at his usual pace and the little guy is falling all over himself tying to keep up. Can you see it? That is what those seven months were like for me. Every day seemed to bring to light another of Linda's issues to deal with. We covered pride, anger, and resentfulness. I can't say I enjoyed the process. As a matter of fact, it was, in essence, like being in hard labor—for seven months—non-stop. With no anesthetic. Yeah!

"Come on, breathe for me," says the doctor.

"Breathe for me? *Breathe for me?* I'll give you breathe for me! How about if you breathe for *me* while my hands are around your neck, choking you? How about that? (Oh, sorry, I must have been having a flashback.) Anyway, you get the picture don't you?

During this time Tom and I were also reconciling. For the first time in my life, my longings were focused on God. So, we could end this story right here and it would be enough,

> All of my past attempts to change failed because I tried to do it in my own strength.

right? It's a beautiful story about how God can work in our lives when we step aside and allow Him to do what *only* He can. All of my past attempts to change failed because I tried to do it in my own strength. I refused to let go. I refused to yield my will to His—and I failed time and again.

Finally, out of sheer desperation I was willing to let Him do whatever was necessary to change me. No strings attached that would allow me to yank it back if the process was too painful or difficult. No matter which road we take, the process is going to be painful. I believe the difference is what happens at the end. What happened at the end of my Kentucky adventure certainly proved that to be true for me.

We had a retreat in the spring, seven months after I arrived there. It was a wonderful time of relaxation and faith sharing. The location, in the foothills of Kentucky, was serene and beautiful. There were volunteers there from several communities. I met Sister Maureen that weekend. She had been volunteering for a month with her sister and was returning home the following week. She was one of those beautiful souls that you gravitate toward. I enjoyed her company during the weekend and hated to tell her goodbye. Tears welled up within me as I told her goodbye and expressed how she would always have a special place in my heart. I would discover later just how profound that statement was. With that, she cupped my face in her hands and tenderly said goodbye. I have never had anyone do that before and there was a surge of energy that went through me that I could not describe. It was an incredible experience and I walked away pondering over and over what that feeling was; a feeling so foreign to me, but so incredible.

The following Sunday, Sister Maureen and some people from her house came to our house to visit. I was so excited, as I thought I would never see her again. When she approached me, she again cupped my face in her hands—and again I had those indescribable feelings. But, alas, after lunch she and her sister headed home.

The next morning, I went to work at the Center, which was connected to the building I lived in. I was usually the first one there. As I opened the door and turned on the lights, there it was on the wall in front of me! You can't see me now as I write these words, but tears are streaming down my cheeks as I recall that moment. On the wall, directly across from me, was the picture of Jesus, perhaps you know it, He is sitting surrounded by children. One little girl is directly in front of Him and He has her face cupped in His hands. When I saw that picture I began to cry uncontrollably. Through Sister Maureen, Jesus showed me how much He loves me. A love I have never before been able to accept. That moment changed my life, like no other. That moment brought a joy into my life that nothing of this world has ever, or will ever, match. The moment when God said, "I love you, My precious child," and my heart could hear it. How about you? Do you truly know that kind of love—that joy that penetrates every fiber of your soul? That love that sustains you in every trial that comes your way? That unconditional love that doesn't say, "your struggles are over." It says, "I will walk through them with you." The love that releases others from impossible demands and allows us to love them, warts and all.

> The love that releases others from impossible demands and allows us to love them, warts and all.

That life-changing experience also brought with it a responsibility. God had done His part. Then He opened the door to a challenge. I had only changed, really changed, if others could see it in the way I lived from that day forward. It is a challenge that I have to renew daily, and it's harder in some areas than others. But, if I am going to call myself a Christian, then I had better act like one—and I had better use God's measuring stick—not the world's.

ARE YOU SET APART?

If you find yourself in the place I once was, the way I see it, you have two choices: you can curse the darkness, or light a candle. When you live for this world, Satan proclaims, "It's my way or the highway." His way is described in Scripture as, *"Now the works of the flesh are evident, which are: adultery, fornication, uncleanness, lewdness, idolatry, sorcery, hatred, contentions, jealousies, outbursts of wrath, selfish ambitions, dissensions, heresies, envy, murders, drunkenness, revelries, and the like; of which I tell you beforehand, just as I also told you in time past, that those who practice such things will not inherit the kingdom of God."*[12] Is there anything ambiguous about these verses? Then why, are we as Christians, just as enmeshed in them as non-Christians?

Some years ago, we had friends who had twin boys. I mean, they were so identical I was never able to tell them apart. Sometimes, one of them would have a cut or scrape that would identify them for a week or two. But other than that it was impossible for me to tell one from the other.

In our society today many Christians and non-Christians are identical twins. You would be hard-pressed to tell the difference and the gap is growing smaller each day. Why? When Jesus was resurrected He instructed His disciples to, *"Go, and make disciples of all nations."*[13] That was the Great Commission. Sadly, over time, the church, right along with society, has "dummied down" that Commission. The non-Christian factions of our society have skillfully redefined morality and Christians are buying into it hook-line-and-sinker. If you shrug your shoulders and exclude yourself from this motley crew because you hold the neutral stance of "tolerance," you are playing with fire. I'm sorry, but you may as well jump into this boiling pot as well, because God also speaks strongly to that position, *"I know your works, that you are neither cold or hot. I could wish you were cold or hot. So then, because you are lukewarm, and neither cold or hot, I will vomit you out of My mouth."*[14] Nothing confusing about that statement.

Tolerance has its place in a pluralistic society, but when it embraces *any* act by *any* person, it becomes a palatable substitute for indifference, or worse, a "get out of jail free" card for our own indiscretions. William Bennett, in his book, *The Death of Outrage,* presents a powerful argument speaking of the Clinton scandal, "This modern allergy to judgments and standards, of which attitudes toward the Clinton scandals are but a manifestation, is deeply problematic, for a defining mark of a good republic is precisely the willingness of its citizens to make judgments about things that matter. In America we do not defer to kings, cardinals, or aristocrats; we rely instead on the people's capacity to make reasonable judgments based on moral principles."[15] It is a provocative book that challenges a stance that God rebukes. A stance that has devastating consequences for individuals and society as a whole—just as devastating as participation in the act itself. And yet, Christians stand shoulder to shoulder with non-believers in the indulgences of, or indifference to, sin. If you really believe "it's all good," everyone has a right to live their life the way they want, no one should impose their moral beliefs on someone else. If you find yourself saying:

"I can't help myself."

"I deserve it."

"If it's good enough for her it's good enough for me."

May I ask you one question? What, in heaven's name did Jesus die for?

Discipleship calls us to a higher purpose. It calls us to boldly proclaim our allegiance to one God, *"you cannot serve two masters."*[16] Dallas Willard speaks of this phenomenon in his book, *The Spirit of The Disciples.* He explains Jesus' intent for His church, "Most problems in contemporary churches can be explained by the fact that members have not yet decided to follow Christ. In the heart of a disciple there is a desire, and there is a decision and settled intent. The disciple of Christ desires above all else, to be like Him. And if we intend to become like Christ, that will be obvious to every thoughtful person around us, as well as ourselves."[17]

Follow Christ or follow the world, you have to decide. These are choices that do not live in harmony. You can do one or the other, but not both. Paul tells the Romans, *"for those who live according to the flesh set their minds on the things of the flesh, but those who live according to the Spirit, the things of the Spirit... Because the carnal mind is enmity against God;.... And those who are in the flesh cannot please God."*[18] The spirit of joy comes from God, not from anything this world has to offer. Following Christ does not bring with it the promise of a trouble-free life filled with joy. That's what we want—and for many, that's as much as we are willing to work for. Which is funny, considering the time and energy we give to worldly pursuits.

And what does that say to young people today? There are frightening statistics that tell us something is wrong: 70 percent of Christian youth leave their faith during college years and never return; suicide is the third leading cause of death among 15-24 year-olds, and the sixth leading cause of death among 5-14 year-olds. We need to ask ourselves why—and what part we play in giving them the message that Christ is not worth following, and life is not worth living?

> The gift, quarried out of the depth of pain and suffering, is the promise of God's love.

Do you walk the walk or simply talk the talk? Do you stand out in a crowd? People are watching, what do they see? Do they see Jesus, or a reflection of themselves? God is watching; does He recognize you as His? The Bible says, "*Do not lay up for yourselves treasures on earth, where moth and rust destroy and where thieves break in and steal; but lay up for yourselves treasures in heaven, where neither moth nor rust destroys and where thieves do not break in and steal. For where your treasure is, there your heart will be.*"[19] What do you treasure?

If you think you have joy, and that joy comes from anything other than God, you have been sold down the River of Deceit by a crafty red-tailed devil. Would you trade a life that seems hopeless at worst and average at best, for a life filled with unimaginable joy? Look at your material possessions for a moment. Do they really make you happy—*really*? God is offering you a treasure for those things you cling to. That treasure is immeasurable joy.

GOD'S TENDER MERCY

When the disciples chose to follow Jesus, their suffering was viewed by some as punishment for sin. You can bet the false prophets of that time jumped on the opportunity to put them on display as a bunch of sinners who were abandoned by God. "Just look at them, it's terrible isn't it? Their sins have brought on all this needless pain and suffering. You know their sins must be terrible because their God has even turned His back on them—pity isn't it?" You may believe the same of your own suffering and could easily fall prey to the belief that God doesn't care about your troubles. That was not true for the disciples and it is not true for us. Scripture says, "*Through the Lord's mercies we are not consumed, because His compassions fail not. They are new every morning. Great is Your faithfulness.*"[20] All through the scriptures, when Peter and Paul speak of their trials, they also speak of God's tender mercies. They never doubted Gods presence in the midst of their trials, or that their trials had a purpose. Suffering without knowing the presence of God is what I did all those years before I allowed Him into my life. Paul wrote, "*Blessed be the God and Father of our Lord Jesus Christ, the Father of mercies and God of all comfort, who comforts us in all our tribulations, that we may be able to comfort those who are in any trouble, with the comfort with which we ourselves are comforted by God. And our hope for you is steadfast, because we know that as you are partakers of the sufferings, so also you will partake of the consolation.*"[21]

> Joy...is peering through tear-stained eyes into an empty tomb.

The gift, quarried out of the depth of pain and suffering, is the promise of God's love and joy for anyone who will step forward and say, "Here I am, Lord."

JOY IS...

The oasis of laughter in the desert of loneliness. It is a caring touch coming through the locked door of a broken heart. It is when your life plays the music of a broken down one-string guitar and God turns it into a symphony. It is peering through tear-stained eyes into an empty tomb.

It is yours for the asking. And at what cost? Well, let's see, you will have to give up a self-centered, self-indulgent, shallow existence. Ewww, that sounds awful. You'll have to bring yourself to the foot of the cross and ask for forgiveness from a merciful God who will cup your face in His hands and call you blessed. Oh—I don't know, maybe you better think about it. *Right!*

So, what do you say? Joy is loving out loud. Are you ready to sing *now*? Someone is watching. "I've got the joy... joy... joy... down in my heart. Hey!

Chapter Three

PEACE

Do you want to be made well?

In John there is a verse that goes like this, *"Now a certain man was there who had an infirmity thirty-eight years. When Jesus saw him lying there, and knew that he already had been in that condition a long time, He said to him, 'Do you want to be made well?"*[1] Can you imagine? "What—are You kidding, Lord?" Of course he wants to be made well. Was Jesus just playing mind games with this poor fellow? No. He wasn't. That was not a rhetorical question He was asking. I know, because He asked me the same thing after many years of suffering. You see, I was so busy trying to live my life under my own will, trying to do it my way, trying to control everything myself, that I didn't feel a need for God.

Even when I did allow God into my life, I didn't give Him control; I just wanted Him to be at my beck and call when things were not going my way. It's kind of like having your own Temp Service. "Hello? Ah—You're there, Lord…good. I was wondering if You could come over about 1:00 am. That's about the time my husband will be stumbling in the door and I thought…well—frankly, I'm at my wits end. Maybe *You* can knock some sense into him."

After years of this, Jesus finally said to me, like the man in John, "Linda, do you really want to be well? Because I can handle those struggles of yours. But, you have to give them all to Me."

It was when I went to Kentucky, at one of the most challenging, hurting, confusing times in my life, that I finally said to God, "Yes, I want to be well." And it was then, when He cupped my face in His hands and said to me, "Linda, you are my beloved child," that I got a glimpse of true peace and its source.

> *Peace does not flow through clenched teeth.*

Sometimes we think we have peace…" Whew, my husband is going fishing with the guys for the weekend. I will have two days of peace!"

"My kids stopped fighting, there's finally peace in the house."

I'm sure you could think of more. A controlling mother-in-law moves out of town. Every year you look forward to the two weeks your tyrant of a boss goes on vacation. That isn't peace. That is the absence of war. True and lasting peace is in the Person of Jesus Christ. We can know it no other way. Can you recognize the difference between a peaceful person and a person who is just stifling their emotions? They attempt to control themselves and give the outward appearance of peace. That's like putting lipstick on a pig. They aren't fooling anyone. Peace does not flow through clenched teeth. Do you know what I'm talking about?

I had a public and private persona. In private everything was out of control. In public I "acted" as though that weren't true. My kids didn't play the game very well though. They would inevitably give us away—usually in church or in the middle of the grocery store. That's were my amateur ventriloquist skills would kick in. Through smiling closed lips and with a death grip on one arm, I would quietly instruct the offender, "you either knock it off or there will be hell to pay when I get you home!" Yeah, peace was flowing like a river!

What takes the place of peace in your life? For me it was anger, fear, a need to control, lack of contentment, and pride.

ANGER: A DOUBLE-EDGED SWORD

I have talked a lot about my anger. As I began this chapter, and made a list of the things that kept me out of God's grace and kept peace out of reach, I revisited all of those angry experiences and frankly, it would be redundant to repeat them here. What I would like to do is ask *you* a few questions. What do you believe about anger—either yours or that of someone you live with or deal with on a regular basis? It is important to know what you believe about it, because that is the basis for how you handle it. Do you believe it is wrong and should never be expressed? Do you believe it is something you can't help, or that it is always justified?

Anger, in and of itself, is not always wrong. If you look through the Old Testament you will see God's anger and wrath is prevalent in some of His dealing with His people. Jesus does not hold back as He deals with the likes of the Pharisees and any of their counterparts who lead God's people astray. It is an emotion God created and it has its purpose. But, there is a fine line between righteous and unrighteous anger and that is what we have to look closely at in our lives. There is a rather obscure book in Scripture, the book of Nahum. Actually, it is only three chapters. But, in *The Message*, in the first chapter it reads, "*He avenges his foes. He stands up against his enemies, fierce and raging. But God doesn't lose his temper. He's powerful, but it's a patient power."*[2]

Many Christians believe that anger is always wrong. If that is true, what do you do with those feelings? If you are a person who never displays anger, I have to ask you, where do you think it goes if you don't deal with it? You may look pretty composed on the outside, but your insides can be like a pressure cooker and eventually they will either explode or implode. Imploding can manifest itself in ailments like ulcers, cancer, a stroke, or heart attack. Somehow, some way, it will rear its ugly head. There is no peace in denial.

There is also no peace in acting out anger, or exploding, when it is unjustified and unrighteous. That is the way I dealt with it. If you don't believe me, I can take you to the last house we lived in. We have only been in our current home for three years, so it hasn't been that long ago. Actually, it was just prior to our separation. In that house, in the kitchen, there is a pantry. On one door of that pantry there is a very large nick. Well, actually the word "nick" gives you too small a picture. Let's call it a gaping hole! What caused that gaping hole was a chair. On the other end of that chair was an out-of-control woman, incredibly frustrated because she wasn't being heard. The chair went flying and for a split-second I had my husband's attention. Not that his hearing improved, or that we resolved anything—but I had his attention—for a second.

So, what *is* the difference between God's righteous anger and my rage that turned a chair into a missile? I'm looking at Scripture and I see words that describe God's anger: He vents His anger; a blaze of anger; fierce anger; the heat of His anger; tremendous anger; burning anger—it's in there, countless situations that provoked Him.

And you know Jesus threw chairs *and* tables when His temple was being used as a "den of thieves." So, why was it okay for Him to throw a chair and not me? Neil Clark Warren, in his book, *Make Anger Your Ally,"* says, "The Bible seems to say that if you could be angry the way God was angry or Jesus was angry, or the prophets were angry, that would be permissible." He contends that, "anger as a response to a violation of essential values is permissible." The difference, he explains, is when our anger turns to aggression, and that aggression is fueled by fear, frustration, or a sense of inadequacy."[3]

> *Anger is not the underlying emotion; it is the outward expression of unmet needs.*

If you are prone to anger or live with someone who is, it is important to understand that anger is learned and can therefore be unlearned. It isn't easy, but it is possible. And the acceptance that it is a learned behavior and not something genetic is important to that process. Anger is not the underlying emotion; it is the outward expression of unmet needs. I truly feel in my heart of hearts that when I realized God's unconditional love for me, the underlying causes of my anger subsided.

WHO'S YOUR BOOGIE MAN?

Growing up, I think I was afraid of everything and acted like I wasn't afraid of anything. When my dad paddled me, I never cried. When my teachers disciplined me, I acted indifferent, I was always in trouble in school.

Back in the "old days" teachers were allowed to inflict corporal punishment, and they did! My first grade teacher would put me under her desk when I misbehaved. Which only gave me a new opportunity to entertain my fan club by sticking my head out from under it and making faces at them. My second grade teacher spanked me, and my third grade teacher whacked me with a ruler on a regular basis. Each consecutive year brought new and different challenges.

I was forever the class clown, never giving away my true identity—that of a frightened child.

I remember sixth grade brought an interesting means of getting attention without enduring physical pain. I would impress my peers with my vast wisdom. It gave me a sense of power and acceptance. Keep in mind now, back then, at the age of 12 or 13, none of us knew anything about anything when it came to sexual matters. But, that didn't make us any less curious, and I quickly recognized our collective need to obtain information in that area. What else could I do, but step in the gap and offer my peers my wealth of knowledge. They were very responsive and eager to learn. At recess we would gather for this continuing education course, provided free of charge, and no-holds-barred. When I think of all those poor minds I warped by fabricating lies to advance my cause—it's rather frightening. For instance, I wonder how many girls became pregnant because I told them that you got that way by kissing a boy when you were menstruating. Somewhere out there, someone is cursing the day they met me! I am truly sorry.

In high school I had to devise more sophisticated stunts to get the attention of others. Besides, trying to crawl out from under a desk may have proved embarrassing to me if I got stuck in the process…it wasn't worth the risk. So, I would defy my teachers at every opportunity and became know as one who would always take a dare. I acquired the reputation for that in the spring of my sophomore year when I dove off a 75-foot cliff —because everyone said I wouldn't. That hurt—my pride *and* my head! I always displayed an air of confidence when I was scared to death. The fear of participating in risky stunts, paled in comparison to the fear I had of being invisible, or having no significance.

Fear went back to college with me last fall. I am currently in my second year of a Deaf Communications Program. It is a dream I have had for a long time and finally realized it was something I was supposed to be doing. But, the idea of returning to school scared me to death. I barely finished high school and because I was married in my junior year, I never considered college an option. That all changed two years ago. In a moment God spoke to my heart and the longing I had to learn sign language resurfaced. Only this time I knew God was behind it. But, as I took that fateful trip down memory lane, the old voices surfaced right out of the gate, trying to convince me that I would never succeed. I went to my first class with much trepidation. I have tried and failed at so many ventures that my family just shrugs their shoulders each time I begin something new. This was a huge commitment, and I was scared. Fear had such a grasp on me that I insisted I had failed every test I took, only to find I did well on each of them.

Finally, I was able to get a grip on myself and realize I had nothing to fear. There is only one thing God tells us to fear— Him! Outside of that He is always telling us not to fear anything:

"Do not fear or be discouraged."[4]

"...then, as the Lord lives, there is safety for you and no harm."[5]

"In God I have put my trust; I will not fear. What can flesh do to me?"[6]

"There is no fear in love; but perfect love casts out fear, because fear involves torment. But he who fears has not been made perfect in love."[7]

The only way of living a fearless life is to be in relationship with God. I have never felt protected by anyone on this earth. It was not until I learned to trust in God's protection

> All the disguises Satan uses to frighten us are exposed and rendered powerless in the light of God's love.

that the truth about fear was brought into the light. All the disguises Satan uses to frighten us are exposed and rendered powerless in the light of God's love.

Have you ever stayed up all night worried and fearful? You can't eat; you can't think; you're irritable, and short-tempered. So, tell me something—how's that working out for you? Did you wake-up one morning and say to yourself, "Whew, my problem is finally solved. Good thing I had the stamina to hang in there until my worrying brought about a resolution." *Right!* God says, "Cut it out!" Jesus asks the question, *"Which of you by worrying can add one cubit to his stature?"*[8]

Peter sure needed a reminder of that the day he stepped out of that boat. The story of Jesus walking on water is in Matthew.[9] The disciples were all in this boat out in the middle of the sea, and the wind and waves were fierce. Suddenly they saw someone walking on the water and they were scared out of their wits. They thought it was a ghost, but Jesus said, "Hey, don't be afraid, it's Me." Peter was impressed, "Hey, I want to try that!" So, Jesus tells him to step out of the boat and Peter does. The scene reminds me of Willey Coyote in the old Road Runner cartoons. He's always chasing the Road Runner who is 100 times faster than him. Inevitably he flies off this cliff and goes airborne, but suddenly realizes where he is and drops like a rock, (don't worry, he never really gets hurt). That's what happened to Peter. He was fine as long as he was focused on Jesus, but as soon as he looked away he sunk and cried out, "Lord, save me!" This is the guy Jesus would give the keys of heaven to! But, on that occasion Peter wasn't trying to impress anyone or save face, he was trying to save his sorry behind. He knew who to call out to when he was in trouble. Fear has no teeth when God is in control.

WAIT A MINUTE—I THOUGHT *I* WAS IN CONTROL

Control was another area of contention for me. The need to rule over everyone was my goal in life: my husband, my kids, and anyone else who wasn't acting according to my rules. My longing to surrender my life to God meant I had to surrender the area of control. That was always God's anyway—who was I kidding? I believe this was the last big battle for me and I went down fighting. God and I were having a tug-of-war with this one, and it has only been recently that He finally won. Of course, when He was skipping off in victory, I had to get in the last word, "Okay, You can have it, I didn't want it anyway!" Do you think there was joy in Mudville that day? You bet. And the cheerleaders were my husband, my adult children, and everyone else who finally got permission to live their own lives.

When we give others that permission, we accept them for who they are. We love them even when they are doing things we don't approve of. It doesn't mean we are not to speak out when someone we love is headed down the wrong path. It means we can't control the outcome. It means we can't hold them down until they cry "uncle." We are to continue to love them even if they reject what we say. Showing them the love of Christ is not possible any other way. And it is the love of Christ alone that will cause lasting change.

CONTENTMENT IS NOT OUT OF REACH

Contentment. Is it really possible to be content in the midst of difficult circumstances? Or does your life have to be perfect first? Do you have to run away from home and responsibilities, and live in seclusion on some primitive island in the Bahamas; eating coconuts and wild berries;

soaking up the sun during the day and tropical breezes at sunset? I'd better stop. This is sounding better all the time! For as long as I can remember, I was never content or satisfied with anything in my life. I never had enough money or clothes; I wasn't smart enough or thin enough; my teeth weren't straight enough; my hair wasn't blonde enough; I wasn't popular enough—blah,blah,blah!

I don't believe in reincarnation, but if I did I would certainly have started out as one of the Israelites. Remember the Israelites? Before God set them free their lives were unbearable under Pharaoh's control. They were oppressed, forced into slave labor, and systematically slaughtered. These were God's chosen people, and after 400 years He had had enough. He would have Moses lead them out of Egypt under His power. But that didn't happen over-night. He didn't just drop Moses out of a tree at Pharaoh's feet. Moses had to grow up into adulthood and then he got sidetracked when he had to escape prosecution for killing an Egyptian. He spent 40 years in exile before God finally called him to set His people free.

The point is, the Hebrews spent all that time as an oppressed people. When they were finally freed, how did they respond to God's work in their lives? Well, it certainly wasn't with peaceful and joyful hearts! Oh, they were singing songs and praising God as they began their journey, and they were very bold. That is until they encountered the Egyptians, in hot pursuit—then the honeymoon was over. They began shaking their fists at Moses saying, *"Because there were no graves in Egypt, have you taken us away to die in the wilderness? Why have you so dealt with us, to bring us up out of Egypt? Is this not the word that we told you in Egypt, saying, 'Let us alone that we may serve the Egyptians?' For it would have been better for us to serve the Egyptians than that we should die in the wilderness."*[10] So, God does that whole parting of the sea and drowning the Egyptians miracle. Now are they content? Sure, until they get thirsty. Whine. Complain.

Okay, Whoosh—the water is sweet and plentiful. Great, are we good to go now? No, now they're hungry. Whine. Complain. Then...

"Look, up in the sky! It's a bird! It's a plane! No, it's manna."

"What's manna?"

"Are we supposed to *eat* this stuff?"

"I *don't* know about the rest of you, but I am really disappointed. This is not what the brochures promised."

"Well, I for one, am ready to go back. At least the Egyptians fed us good while we suffered."

Poor Moses, he was always on the receiving end of their *bellyaching*. How frustrating it must have been for him. Each time God responded to their cries of indignation, just to have them come up with something new that caused them to long for the good old days of slavery and oppression. They never seemed to be satisfied. And they stayed in the desert a *long* time because of their incessant whining and complaining.

I too spent a long time in the desert, and it wasn't fun. But for some reason, when I was in the midst of it, I couldn't see it for what it was. I had to have things. We had a beautiful home, new cars, a swimming pool, and shopping was my favorite past time. When I was upset, sad, or feeling rejected, I would take my pity party shopping and buy a new outfit, or two, or three. Occasionally, I would throw in a little trinket for my husband so I wouldn't feel guilty. He was never allowed to buy me clothes for Christmas or my birthday because he would not buy name brands, and I *had* to have name brands! Besides anyone who would get upset because his polyester leisure suit was sold in a garage sale— would not be shopping for me. Period!

Our inability to be content is like a dog continuously chasing his tail. The world has made contentment an action word. We need to go *get* contentment. We need to aspire to the world's idea of success so we can acquire all the material things that will satisfy us. But, in reality that will never happen. The top of the corporate ladder is crowded with disenchanted dreams and expectations. There is absolutely nothing of this world that will bring us contentment. Because of that—peace will always be out of our reach. Covetousness is the prodigal son of peace. Who do you suppose the companion and best friend of covetousess is? Pride.

"PRIDE GOES BEFORE DESTRUCTION"[11]

The same lies that keep contentment at bay, give pride a respectable face. Some people would believe that pride really isn't so bad. Is there something wrong with telling someone we are proud of them, or perhaps we are proud of ourselves for some accomplishment? What's wrong with that? It appears so innocent that we can fail to understand why God considers it such an awful sin. Who are we kidding when

> *The same lies that keep contentment at bay, give pride a respectable face.*

we get all puffed up about ourselves? Pride is comparing; it is saying I am better than someone else. If I have money, pride says I have more money than you. If I am attractive, pride says I am more attractive than you. If I am successful, pride says I am better and smarter than you. It certainly is not a sin to have money, or be attractive or successful, if we realize those things are a gift from God. The sin is in patting *ourselves* on the back for something God has done—to glorify ourselves and not Him. That's why God *hates* pride. Proverbs shows God's feelings clearly, *"The fear of the Lord is to hate evil; pride and arrogance and the evil way and the perverse mouth I hate."*[12]

Satan has brilliantly disguised pride—the foundation of all sins. He knows it well, since it was what caused his fall from

God's grace. But he didn't start out that way. Ezekiel 28:12-15 says of Satan, "*You were the seal of perfection, full of wisdom and perfect in beauty. You were in Eden, the garden of God; Every precious stone was your covering; The sardius, topaz, and diamond, beryl, onyx, and jasper, sapphire, turquoise, and emerald with gold. The workmanship of your timbrels and pipes was prepared for you on the day you were created. You were the anointed cherub who covers; I established you; you were on the holy mountain of God; you walked back and forth in the midst of fiery stones. You were perfect in your ways from the day you were created. Till iniquity was found in you.*"[13]

Then he fell from God's grace, "*By the abundance of your trading you became filled with violence within and you sinned... Your heart was lifted up because of your beauty. You corrupted your wisdom for the sake of your splendor...All who knew you among the peoples are astonished at you. You have become a horror, and shall be no more forever.*"[14]

He watched and waited—when he first began his quest to bring down all of God's people he didn't have much to work with. I wonder what he did to entertain himself for the first few hundred years of creation. While God was busy creating His beautiful children and a glorious garden for them to live in, Satan was chewing at the bit to put his newfound skills to work. No sooner did God leave the garden than Satan slithered up to Eve. He wanted to know just what God had told her. She tells him, "*...We may eat the fruit of the trees of the garden; but of the fruit of the tree which is in the midst of the garden, God has said, 'You shall not eat it, nor shall you touch it, lest you die.*'"[15] They had free access to everything in the garden, except for that one stinking apple tree. I'll bet it didn't even appeal to them when God first pointed it out.

Then Satan masterfully cast every doubt in their minds about God's true purpose in obeying Him. "Come on, you don't believe all that stuff, do you? God didn't really mean you would *die* if you ate the fruit. You misunderstood Him.

What He *really* meant was, if you eat of the fruit in the midst of the garden, *"your eyes will be opened and you will be like God, knowing good and evil."*[16] You can be your very own god—just like me! Do you think the pride that caused Adam and Eve to fall from God's grace brought them any peace? Do you believe Satan has *ever* known peace? Anyone who roams the earth like a roaring lion all day long couldn't possibly have any peace.

Pride is a lot of work. Did you ever play "king of the hill" when you were a child? When I was young, there was only one girl who lived near me, and my mother wouldn't let me play with her, that left only friends of my brothers. My mother would push me out the back door and tell my brother to play with me. Oh, they played with me all right! They beat me up, threw me on the ground and piled on top of me, threw things at me; and anything else they could dream up, until I had had enough and went inside.

So, anyway…"king of the hill." I would manage to get on top of the hill for a millisecond. That's all I lasted before some big, ugly boy would knock me off. That's what it's like with pride. You want to be king of the hill, but you constantly have to be protecting your place. It's a lot of work.

I would be lying if I said I have completely obliterated pride from my life. But, something that I found fascinating is that it wasn't until I began writing this book that I truly discovered that I have nothing to be prideful or boastful about. God certainly moved me along that path when I was in Kentucky, but as I began to realize that God was calling me to write this book I fell flat on my face in amazement. You would think that just the opposite would happen—that it would cause me to get all puffed up and more prideful. But, the opposite is true and I think it is because this was so big! There was no way for me to keep a poker face that simply said, "Awe, heck, it was nothing." I never would have imagined in my wildest dreams, that I could do this. And that truth, instead of puffing me up and moving me to dedicate a shrine to myself, brought me to my knees.

I often think of Jesus and the fact that He told His disciples He could do nothing and was nothing without God. That is so difficult for me to comprehend because Jesus *is* God. Now, I am not a theologian and don't pretend to be, but when I contemplate that, I understand that in the spiritual realm Jesus is God, but when He came to earth He became human. It is this human side that speaks to His

> *Pride is your refusal to be yourself before God.*

total dependence on God. At least that is how I see it, and knowing that humbles me. If the perfect human is totally dependent on God who am I kidding, acting like I am something I am not—strutting around like God comes to me for advice! I heard recently that pride is your refusal to be yourself before God.

Perhaps that is why God hates pride so much—because pride tells God we are not satisfied with the person He created. We are not satisfied with what our blessed, glorious, magnificent God has created? My friends do you see this tear-stained page? Pride is a slap in God's face and the tears are not only His, but mine as well, because as I write this—that profound truth has just pierced my heart.

SCRIPTURE AND PRAYER, THE KEYS TO PEACE

If you also long for peace in your life, God wants you to know something. He tells us what keeps us from living a peaceful life and He shows us how to find it, *"Where do wars and fights come from among you? Do they not come from your desires for pleasure that war in your members? You lust and do not have. You murder and covet and cannot obtain. You fight and war. Yet you do not have because you do not ask. You ask*

*and do not receive, because you ask amiss, that you may spend
it on your pleasures. Adulterers and Adulteresses! Do you not
know that friendship with the world is enmity with God?
Whoever therefore wants to be a friend of the world makes himself an enemy of God.*

*Therefore submit to God. Resist the devil and he will flee
from you. Draw near to God and He will draw near to you.
Cleanse your hands, you sinners; and purify your hearts, you
double-minded. Lament and mourn and weep! Humble yourselves in the sight of the Lord, and He will lift you up."*[17]

Later, God tells us how to find the peace we long for
through prayer. *"Is anyone among you suffering? Let him
pray…The effective fervent prayer of a righteous man avails
much."*[18] I have found that the two disciplines I began earnestly
in Kentucky, prayer and reading God's Word, have been the
catalyst to my relationship with Him, which, in turn, has
brought me peace. Although I have done both for many years,
it has not been with such a longing as I have now—to really
know God and to surrender my will to His. How is it possible
to be in such a place and not *know* that person? It isn't.

You may never meet me, but when you finish this book
you will know a lot about me, right? If we meet and become
friends that brings us to a whole new level. That is how God's
Word and prayer bring us into relationship with Him.
Talking to God and reading Scripture everyday has brought
me to a place I never before imagined. Little by little, He has
drawn me away from worldly desires and closer to Him. Step
by step, He has given me tasks and challenges to overcome,
but He is there all the while, guiding me. Paul tells us, *"Be
anxious for nothing, but in everything by prayer and supplica-
tion, with thanksgiving, let your requests be made known to
God; and the peace of God, which surpasses all understanding,
will guard your hearts and minds through Christ Jesus."*[19]

In the past my prayers were shallow and demanding. I
would continually ask God to do specific things: change my

circumstances, change other people, make my life easier—it wasn't about surrendering to God's will, it was about changing God's will to conform to mine. I have a daily journal titled, "Experiencing God Day-By-Day." This is what it says about prayer, "Prayer is not designed to change God, it is designed to change us. Prayer is not calling God in to bless our activities. Rather, prayer takes us into God's presence, shows us His will, and prepares us to obey Him." When Jesus was going to the cross He prayed that God would take the cup from Him, but ended His prayer saying, *"Not my will but Yours be done."*[20]

Our lives must be aligned with God's will, if we are to experience the fruits of prayer. As I have surrendered more of my will to His, He has revealed Himself more and more to me in ways that quite simply blow me away. Let me give you an example. My son Shawn, who is in the Army, was sent to Afghanistan last summer. When he first went I was very concerned and determined that I would fast one day a week for whatever length of time he was gone. Now let me tell you, fasting is a very difficult discipline for me, and one that I am not very good at. So, I decided that would be a special way to pray for him. Also, I began to think that some things I once considered important, in light of my son's being in harms way, became trivial. Pat on the back and off I went.

Then God stopped me dead in my tracks! One morning I was running—one of my favorite times to converse with God. Something had happened before I left that would normally have upset me, but having this new attitude helped me get over it. As I was running and praying, my commitment to Shawn was brought to mind and suddenly God said to me clearly and unmistakably, "What about Me? I gave up My Son to death—for you! Yet you will fast for your son, and not for Me?" I got a vivid picture of Jesus on the cross and I lost it right there. I could not control the tears or the sorrow for having offended God.

I have had other experiences like that in the past few years. Could that have happened in the past, when I was not in relationship with Him? There's no way that would have been possible, and it is only in that deep relationship that I have come to grow in surrender and peace. I began this chapter at that time because I was dealing with a situation in my home that was very difficult for me. It was a litmus test for just how peaceful my life is right now. I am happy to report, that even though the circumstances have not changed, I have remained steadfast. That has only been possible by my giving my worries to God and *believing* He will take care of them.

One of my favorite prayers, which hangs right here where I can see it every day, is the Serenity Prayer: "God grant me the serenity to accept the things I cannot change, courage to change the things I can, and wisdom to know the difference." The wisdom comes from God through Scripture—make time to read it. Serenity that comes from knowing God is only a prayer away—talk to Him. As He was preparing to go to the cross, one of the last things Jesus said to His disciples was, *"Peace I leave with you, My peace I give to you; not as the world gives do I give to you."*[21] True and lasting peace can only be found through Christ.

Chapter Four

PATIENCE

"...with patience, bearing with one another in love"[1]

Knowing I was preparing for this chapter I told myself I had better practice this virtue of which I struggle within some areas myself. My most difficult challenge is behind the wheel of my car. For some reason, wherever I am going I have a sense I have to get there fast. Two years ago, I was diagnosed with ADHD. Do you know the two things they say you should never give to someone with ADHD? A loaded gun and the keys to a car. I can tell you from personal experience, both are true!

I want it to be known that my type of driving does not constitute road rage. That is something far different than what I am speaking of. Road rage is a terrible phenomenon of today's culture. People everywhere are stressed and angry and looking for someone to direct that anger toward—be it on the road or elsewhere. They are out for Number One and dare anyone to get in their way.

But when I get behind the wheel of my car I am on a mission, no matter where I am going, and have one-sided conversations with people who have the misfortune of getting in front of me. I have a lot of patience with people behind me—but little for those in front of me. You'll be happy to know I am working on it. I now try to realize that nothing I do will change them, so why allow them to upset me? This attitude could be considered patience. But not the patience God calls us to in Scripture—it goes much deeper than that. It goes to the One whose immeasurable patience continually returns forgiveness and mercy for our sins.

GOD...OUR MODEL OF PATIENCE

Beth Moore, in her Bible study, "Living Beyond Yourself," says, "the Greek word makrothumia is translated into the English word "patience," and the Greek word hupomone is translated into the English word "endurance." By using both of these words, Paul emphasized the importance of being patient in respect to persons, and enduring in respect to situations or circumstances."[2]

> Patient endurance
>
> It is the longing for relationship that looks beyond the deliverer of biting words or hateful actions to the Deliverer of souls.

Patient endurance is also known as longsuffering—one of the qualities which is supposed to distinguish Christians from others. It is the attitude that enables one to bear hurt without retaliation—the ability to come face to face with anger, and return love. It is the longing for relationship that looks beyond the deliverer of biting words or hateful actions to the Deliverer of souls.

The degree of patience we are to model in our circumstances and our relationships we learn from the Creator of patience—Our Lord. He shares a parable of that lesson in Matthew. I will paraphrase it for you. There was a king who decided one day to settle all of his accounts with his servants. One servant in particular was called in to settle his debt of ten thousand talents. That was an enormous amount of money. He knew there was no way to pay the debt, and the king was prepared to have him sold with his wife, children, and all of his belongings. The servant fell to his knees and begged for the king's mercy and patience. The king looked at his sorry state, and without a second thought, forgave the entire debt. The servant stood up, brushed himself off, and no doubt in somewhat of a daze, headed out the door.

Imagine that! Surely this guy would have been elated, and would have spent much of the rest of his existence in a state of gratitude. He must have run home kissed his wife and kids and shared the blessing with them. Well, that's not quite how the story ends. It seems our friend had a short memory…and a short fuse. Scripture says he "went out and found" a fellow servant who owed him a hundred denarii, a very small amount of money. He didn't just stumble across the guy, he went searching for him, and when he caught up with him he took him by the jugular and demanded his money. The second servant did exactly what the first servant did just moments before—he begged for patience and mercy. But, unlike the king, our friend refused and had him thrown in prison.

Little did he know that they would soon be cellmates when the king found out. The king was angry and had the servant brought back to him, *"You wicked servant! I forgave you all that debt because you begged me. Should you not have had compassion on your fellow servant, just as I had pity on you?"* And off to jail he went.[3]

I have seen the difference between ten thousand talents and 100 denarii described this way: 100 denarii could have been carried in a pocket. It was one five-hundred thousandth of the debt which the first servant owed. In comparison, ten thousand talents cashed into denarii would require some 25,000 men carrying sacks stuffed with denarii over their shoulders. Standing in a line about a yard apart, they would stretch out for about 20 miles.

God used this example to show us the enormous capacity of His patience and mercy for us, compared to the paltry amount required of us, when dealing with people and circumstances in our lives. He knew there was no way the first servant could possibly have repaid that debt if the king had demanded it of him, and likewise, there is no way for us to repay the debt we owe Him. A debt God has also forgiven. Should our compassion, patience, and forgiveness toward others be any less?

> *Is God's patience not on display for us every time we sin against Him—every time we forget His mercies and treat others badly?*

Is God's patience not on display for us every time we sin against Him—every time we forget His mercies and treat others badly? It seems I am committing the same sins over and over again. Each time I stand before God I feel as though I will never overcome them. Like Paul, I continue to do the things I hate.[4]

Paul tells the Romans, *"Or do you presume on the riches of His kindness and forbearance and patience, not knowing that God's kindness is meant to lead you to repentance?"*[5] God can't help being kind and patient, that's who He is, and because of that I am able to go to Him no matter how many times it takes to get it right.

I was just wondering about our friend, Jonah. What do you think? Do you think God's patience rubbed off on him?

It doesn't appear that way. When he ran away, God caught up with him after the fishermen threw him over board. God said to him, "Okay, buddy you want a place to hide from Me? I'll give you a place to hide!" Our whale friend got a tasty little delicacy, and Jonah had three days and three nights to ponder his fate. He was sorry, he changed his mind—and he stunk to high heaven. God's praises echoed all through that massive cavity he inhabited. God instructed the whale to turn him loose, and Jonah washed ashore.

It is so typical of us, isn't it? What was true for Jonah, was also true for me. "Oh God! If you'll just get me out of this one, I promise I'll _____." How quickly we forget. How quickly we convert back to our old ways. But God is patient and loving, and he forgives again and again. Why?

When I was growing up I lied to my parents at every opportunity. Would I have ever considered going to them and telling them I messed up? What—are you kidding me? I knew what that meant.

"Gordie, (that's my dad), your daughter needs a spanking!"

"Linda," my dad would shout, "Go get me the paddle."

I would go out to the utility room, open the closet door, stare at that nicely edged and varnished, 1/2" thick piece of behavior modification, and shout back to my dad, "I can't find it!"

My indiscretions were always met with unmerciful spankings—why wouldn't I lie? I liked to play the odds. I didn't get caught *every time* and when I did, well, a beating was a beating. It wouldn't have gone easier on me if I would have been honest up front and begged for mercy. So, I learned early on to lie about everything that had the slightest possibility of sending me to the utility room—and deny the rest. If God dealt with us that way would we run to Him so readily to repent? Not me, thank you very much.

Another example I recall is when I took Home Economics in High School. We were learning to sew. I purchased a blouse pattern and material, and was working on it at home. My mother knew how to sew, so when I ran into a problem I asked her for help. She grew impatient with me in short order because I failed to understand her instructions. So, she grabbed it away from me and began to do it herself. I explained to her that I had to do it. She walked off in a huff and after that I refused to ask her for any more advise.

There was a problem with that though, I had no idea what I was doing and had to bring the finished product to class the next day. What I presented to my teacher was the end result of a frustrated effort. One sleeve was inside out, the zipper was sewn shut, and the whole thing was two sizes too small. That was the result of trying to do it myself, instead of asking for help from an impatient and demanding parent.

But the results are much different with God and that is exactly why God is so patient with us. Because if He were not, we would be afraid of Him and not trust in Him. It would be easier to do it ourselves, and don't we usually mess things up when we do that?

There are also others watching. If my friends saw how my mother treated me when I was trying to learn from her, would they go to her for help? Of course not. God longs for us to trust in Him and come to Him for everything. He longs to shower us with blessings and guide us through all the obstacles this world presents to us.

When I first began my walk with God, and for many years after, I found it very difficult to accept that He could be so patient. That wasn't what I was used to and I continually failed Him. I just kept waiting for the ax to fall. I found it hard to turn to Him when I failed so miserably because I was sure what was waiting for me when I walked in the door: the disapproval, the cursing, the spanking, the reminder that I was "bad." But, *that* was my experience with my earthly parents, not my heavenly Father. How awesome it was when I discovered that I could reach out to Him in repentance, and have assurance of forgiveness—all from a loving and patient Father.

There is a verse in Psalms that speaks of the Israelites and their journey in the desert. Remember their constant complaining? *"They soon forgot His works; they did not wait for His counsel."*[6] It is our impatience with God, with ourselves and others, that is the stumbling block to our walk with Him. And that stumbling block will cause others to stumble as well.

I think about how long God waited for me to turn to Him. All the years I lived in sin and opposition to His will, defying Him at every turn. Then many more years after I called myself a Christian— still living by my own rules and desires—calling upon Him when it was convenient or when I was desperate. And there He was, patiently waiting for me. Matthew says, *"Ask, and it will be given to you; seek and you will find; knock and it will be opened to you."*[7] God says, "Just ask and it's yours, that's how much I love you. As a matter of fact, I love you *so* much that I am going to do something for you that you could or would never ask for *and* I'm going to do it even while you are still sinning and denying Me. I am going to sacrifice My own Son, so you, little Miss Sinner, will have eternal life. Then I am going to wait patiently for you to return to Me. And that's not all. Every time you ask sincerely, I will forgive you." God is patient because of His great mercy and love for us. He does not want even one to perish.

> *I am going to sacrifice My own Son, so you, little Miss Sinner, will have eternal life. Then I am going to wait patiently for you to return to Me.*

JESUS LIVED WHAT GOD SPOKE

You want to talk about patience? How about Jesus? If God came to me and said, "Linda, I have a special job for you. You've been pretty good about small tasks I have given you, so I have something bigger. I want you to go save the world and you have three years to do it. Good luck and keep Me posted." Poof—He's gone. After the initial shock wears off, I panic. "Okay, okay. I can do this. Okay, where do I start? Okay, get a grip Linda. Okay—a plan, I need a plan. Three years—okay, where do I start? I'll have to stop eating, that takes time, and then I'll have to cut back to 4 hours sleep a night, and let's see…okay, people—I need to reach all those people. NOW! I need to do it NOW! No time to waste." Does that sound about right to you? Well, not to Jesus. I guess that's why God sent Him and not me. Lucky you.

Jesus knew His assignment well. He knew what was expected of Him, and He knew how much time He had. None of it was a surprise. Yet, He never panicked and never spent time drawing up plans and charts and maps. Did you ever see Him rush anywhere? Did you ever see anything that remotely resembled impatience? No, you didn't. (Well, maybe with those arrogant religious leaders, but that was justified.) As a matter of fact, it amazes me that when Jesus began His ministry the first thing the Holy Spirit did was send Him into the desert for forty days to be tempted by Satan. I had to ask the question: why is He wasting so much time? Thirty years has passed already, and now He's going to spend 40 days in the desert? Let's get busy already.

Many times Jesus is shown retreating to pray in the midst of throngs of people gathered to hear Him preach. And He didn't wait until He had crowds of people gathered before He preached. I mean, if you don't have much time, wouldn't you spend it with as many people as possible. Let's fill a stadium, for heaven's sake. But, He actually gave His best sermons to individuals: the woman at the well, the guy in the tree, the lone leper. He left a crowd to go the Zacchaeus' house for dinner. Come on, some good time-management may have been in order here.

What was He thinking? Do you really want to know? He tells us not to worry about anything, and not to seek after things that don't matter. *"But seek the kingdom of God, and all these things shall be added to you."*[8] The Gospels, which tell of Jesus' short time here and His ministry, speak of how His main focus was on His total reliance on, and His relationship with, His Father. A relationship fostered by prayer. There was no need to hurry about the business of salvation. When you read about His manner it is always that of peace, patience, and confidence. Nowhere do you find Him rushing from speaking engagement to speaking engagement. There was no schedule, no agenda, and amazingly—no stress.

Jesus was not only patient with His time, He was also patient with His followers. They seemed to be pretty slow learners, and they spent a lot of time in a blurry haze of confusion. Not only confusion about Jesus' purpose, but also their own. They regressed a lot and backed off when the kitchen heated up. But, Jesus remained a steadfast teacher. Not like any teacher I ever had, that's for sure.

At first glance, it may seem that Jesus could have started sooner or spent less time alone and more time preaching. But, we fail to see God's perfect plan in His Son's life as well as our own. Jesus waited patiently for God to direct His every step. He never lost His focus, and regardless of how it looks, He never wasted a moment's time. On the cross when He uttered those final words, *"It is finished,"*[9] it was. Everything was checked off the list and He went home. There was nothing left undone. Or was there?

WORK UNDONE?

Was Jesus finished? Yes, *He* was finished. But there was work still to be done. And…the rest was left to His followers—work to be accomplished by the power of the Holy Spirit. That great commission continues to the end of time.

> The patience of God and Jesus Christ should be the hallmark of every Christian intent on bringing others to the throne of God.

And the patience of God and Jesus Christ should be the hallmark of every Christian intent on bringing others to the throne of God. And like Jesus, we must wait patiently for God to direct our steps and patiently deal with our circumstances, ourselves, and those in our lives.

Scripture tells what patience is all about as it is related in *The Message*; *"Meanwhile, friends, wait patiently for the Master's Arrival. You see farmers do this all the time, waiting for their valuable crops to mature, patiently letting the rain do its slow but sure work. Be patient like that. Stay steady and strong. The Master could arrive at any time. Friends, don't complain about each other. A far greater complaint could be lodged against you, you know. The Judge is standing just around the corner. Take the old prophets as your mentors. They put up with anything, went through everything, and never once quit, all the time honoring God. What a gift life is to those who stay the course! You've heard, of course, of Job's staying power, and you know how God brought it all together for him at the end. That's because God cares, cares right down to the last detail."*[10]

ARE WE A STUMBLING BLOCK FOR OTHERS?

I am continually having to ask myself, "Am I helping God or standing in His way? If I call myself a Christian and I am impatient and judgmental, am I negatively influencing a searcher? Do I douse the embers of a questioning heart with the waters of criticism? Paul says, *"Therefore let us not judge one another anymore, but rather resolve this, not to put a stumbling block or a cause to fall in our brother's way."*[11]

> Do I *douse the embers of a questioning heart with the waters of criticism?*

Don't we keep score? I did this for you and in return I expect something of equal or greater value from you? The Bible tells us differently, *"...freely you have received, freely give."*[12] Here is the basis upon which we should exercise patience, love, and kindness toward our fellow sinners—not judgment.

Today patience is a dinosaur, and if perseverance doesn't come in pill form, we aren't interested. It's true everywhere we look. I want it now, I don't want to have to wait for it, I don't want to feel it, I don't want to deal with it. Give me another credit card—a pill—or a bus ticket out of here. Just give me something *now!* We have no patience with our circumstances or the people around us. We are even impatient with God.

Romans tells us, *"Oh, the depth of the riches both of the wisdom and knowledge of God! How unsearchable are His judgments and His ways past finding out. For who has known the mind of the Lord? Or who has become His counselor? Or who has first given to Him and it shall be repaid to him?"*[13] I don't recall God ever asking me for advice. How about you?

"Okay Lord, I am going to give this situation to you, please do something. Oh—sorry. You weren't fast enough. I'll have to take it back and deal with it myself." What arrogance to put our timetable on God's perfect plan. What if someone other than God had been in charge of my salvation? "All right Linda you have until 5:00 P.M., June 4, 1987 to get yourself saved. After that, the gates close, and you are out of luck." That's not how God works, but it's how we humans work. And—it *doesn't* work. But we fail again and again to learn the lesson.

1 Timothy in *The Message* reads, *"Here's a word you can take to heart and depend on: Jesus Christ came into the world to save sinners. I'm proof—Public Sinner Number One—of someone who could never have made it apart from sheer mercy. And now he shows me off—evidence of his endless patience—to those who are right on the edge of trusting him forever."*[14] You see, my past miserable life had a purpose: for others who struggle to see the awesomeness of a God who doesn't give up on us. Amazing Grace!

How many times, though only in hindsight, have you seen God's perfect plan in your own life? For me, it has been often. I would have a situation I was concerned about and then develop a picture in my mind of the solution. Then as I would pray for that situation, I would interject my solution, just in case God didn't have one Himself. Later, after the situation was resolved, God's way of course, I would stand in awe of His methods and ways. "Wow! I never thought of that. You're good." To think I would have the *audacity* to give God advice.

But, that's what we do with our impatience and the thorn in our side. Not Paul. He acknowledged the thorn in his side. Which, although we are not told what it was, we certainly are clear that it was something painful and something he hated.[14] But, it was God's way of keeping Paul reliant on Him. How is He keeping us reliant on Him? A husband who refuses to change, a child who is headed down a path of destruction and tells you to butt out of their life, a physical or emotional pain that lingers? There are countless ways we struggle and grow impatient with people and circumstances and the answer is always the same: it's not about me—it's about God. So, let go and let God.

And what about those people in our lives who we have dedicated ourselves to saving? They have somehow, by birth or accident, stumbled into our lives and messed up in some way, and we are on a crusade to snatch their wretched souls from hell and damnation. No time to waste. But God says, "Cut it out. You are trespassing." When we take it upon ourselves to control or manipulate someone else's life, we are interfering with God's plan and He doesn't like it. As well intentioned as we may be, we could actually be pushing them further away from God.

PERSISTENCE IS THE ACTIVITY OF PATIENCE

There is a story about Thomas Edison. A reporter once asked him, "Mr. Edison, why have you failed 2,000 times perfecting the light bulb?" Thomas Edison replied, "I did not fail, it took 2,000 steps to perfect it." How about that for persistence?

Many people view patience as a weakness. As if it means to simply kick back and stay out of God's way. Or it can be an excuse to not be involved in the process. But, patience is to be balanced with persistence. Before I understood and bought into this virtue of patience, I was hell on wheels. I was on a mission to "fix" everyone around me, and there was no time to waste. Oh, I would make a superficial effort to change my own ways, but that was secondary to my real calling—to change everyone else in my life, for their own good, of course.

If they would make an effort, it wasn't good enough. If they fell back, it wasn't acceptable. And watch out if they chose to ignore my guidance *all together*. But, I was the proverbial clashing cymbal—making a lot of noise, but producing no fruit. It has only been recently that I have truly begun to change. It wasn't a throw-my-hands-up-and-walk-away change. It wasn't a change that declared, "these people are hopeless why am I bothering?" It was a revelation that there is a God and it isn't me. Thank God! The *real* God is patient beyond measure, and loves without condition. And He is persistent. He doesn't force His way into our lives, but that nudging at our hearts—that's Him: standing in the doorway, peeking in the window; waving His hands wildly to get our attention—until we acknowledge Him. Then He rejoices.

That is our model of how to treat ourselves and others. My driving force is now prayer, and I love the example of the persistent widow. In *The Message,* Jesus told people a story showing that it was necessary for them to pray consistently and never quit. He said, *"There was once a judge in some city who never gave God a thought and cared nothing for people. A widow in that city kept after him: 'My rights are being violated, protect me!' He never gave her the time of day. But after this went on and on he said to himself, 'I care nothing what God thinks, even less what people think. But because this widow won't quit badgering me, I'd better do something and see that she gets justice—otherwise I'm going to end up beaten black and blue by her pounding. Then the Master said, 'Do you hear what that judge, corrupt as he is, is saying? So what makes you think God won't step in and work justice for his chosen people, who continue to cry out for help?'* "[15]

And while you're at it, be persistent in love as well, *"Let all that you do be done in love."*[16] Nagging, cajoling, and forcing your will on others is not God's way, nor is it His desire. We may not be privy to His plan, but we know His desire.

So, keep asking, and it will be given to you. Keep seeking, and you will find. Keep knocking, and it will be opened to you. Keep doing it your way and you lose—and so does everyone else in your life.

Chapter Five

KINDNESS
& GENTLENESS

"Love requires no sacrifice but of our own selfish natures."

Nancy G. Danforth[1]

Kindness and gentleness are virtues that I struggled with for years, because frankly, I had never experienced such things in my own life. So that, get-them-before-they-get-you mentality was always my frame of reference. If you didn't give me a reason to not like you, I could dream one up. For so many years, I harbored anger and resentment and responded to others in very unkind ways, and there was nothing gentle about my manner of doing it. But, I always felt I had a right—people had hurt me, and I felt they deserved to be hurt in return. That kind of defensive, self-serving attitude leaves little, if any, room for God. True loving kindness begins with God, moves into self, and then reaches out to others. Virtues like kindness and gentleness cannot take root in a hardened heart.

I want to tell you a story of how God taught me a power-ful lesson concerning my unkind, and not so gentle ways—and at the same time, dispel any assumptions that God does not have a sense of humor.

When I was in Kentucky, I was the House Manager of the building in which twelve to fifteen volunteers lived. One of my jobs was to control spending. We were to be good stew-ards of the money allocated to our community.

The building we lived in was an old motel. Our commu-nity area was a large living room, a kitchen and a dining area. This part of the building had it's own heating and cooling system. One morning, in late summer, I walked into the liv-ing room and noticed immediately that it was freezing. When I checked the thermostat, the temperature was 65. I was upset that someone would do that when no one was in that part of the building all night. It was a terrible waste of money and I went immediately into my 'I'm going to find out who did this and teach them a lesson mode.' I reset the thermostat to 75, duct taped the cover shut, and left a huge note on the board in the kitchen, "Whoever is resetting the thermostat, please stop, blah, blah, blah."

The next morning, I found the thermostat back on 65. I was livid. I put more tape on the cover and left a nastier note in the kitchen. Everyone acted as though they had no idea who was resetting it every night. But, alas, I was sure I knew.

Every evening after dinner we had devotionals and it hap-pened that it was my turn to plan that evening's. I spent much of the day preparing it, gathering Scripture verses and letters from elderly contributors that read something like this, "I am an 85 year-old widow on social security. I have no family left. My only companion, my beloved cat, drowned in a cistern, and my electric has been shut off. But I am sending you $5.00. It isn't much, but it is all I have." There, that should do it.

During the devotional I did not divulge the fact that I knew who the culprit was, but I couldn't resist the opportunity to send dirty looks her way. When we were finished, I went to my room, resting in the confidence that I had skillfully resolved the problem and that, although she didn't admit to anything, surely she learned a lesson.

The next morning, as I entered the living room, I was aghast at the realization that all was in vain because the temperature was again 65. I lunged at the thermostat and suddenly my eyes fell on something that I had not noticed before. It was a set-back thermostat. The temperature was set on 65 and each time I manually set it at 75, it automatically returned to 65. I was an idiot and God was loving it. I'm sure of it. He was loving his creative lesson plan and he was loving my reaction. Never before had I gotten such a clear picture of how badly I treated other people, or how much I was trying to hide my brokenness.

Charles Stanley, in his book, *The Blessings of Brokenness,* explains the reason we struggle so with gentleness. "Being unbroken we turn to other people. We demand that they love us, provide for us, and meet all of our emotional needs. We discover that other people fail us as much as we fail ourselves. They are unreliable. So, we resent them, are angry with them, and feel bitter and frustrated and disappointed by them. We then act in very ungentle, abusive, and unkind ways toward them."[2]

Well, that described me to a "T." Anyone who didn't conform to my demands and rules would suffer my wrath, and, of course, my family took the brunt of it. In particular, my daughter Wendy, who was seven when Tom and I were married. I was pregnant by the following March and our three boys arrived very close together. Wendy felt pushed aside and I was too busy to notice. I remember responding to her protests by expecting her to realize, as if she were an adult, that babies had physical demands that needed to be met. It wasn't that I loved them more. I was unable to recognize or respond to her emotional needs, which were just as important.

Actually, I became verbally and physically abusive to her as I clung, with a tenuous grip, to a life out of control.

I was struggling in every area of my life and lashed out at anyone I felt was causing *me* pain. But even in the midst of all that—God was speaking to me. I began praying and reading Scripture. A friend told me about a radio program, "Focus On The Family." I will forever be indebted to Dr. James Dobson and his ministry, for the many programs and books that literally taught me to be a better person and parent.

Change came so slowly, but God was persistent. My problem was that I skipped over a very essential part of the process. I was trying to be kind to others, but could not receive it myself, especially from God. That caused me to fall back a lot. I was so frustrated each time I failed—I couldn't understand why it was so hard. I made gradual progress and began to try to heal relationships, especially with my daughter. I longed to receive her forgiveness, but because of the missing puzzle piece, change was slow and forgiveness would take time.

Looking back, I realize that all my efforts were external. I was sincere about my desire to change, that wasn't the problem. The problem was that I was trying to do it under my own strength. What that gives you is a better-than-nothing result. I have an analogy for you (don't roll those eyes at me!). I have two rose bushes in my yard. I am looking at them right now. I love roses, but I stink at growing them. The branches are massive and beautiful, but there has never been one single bud all summer. Not one! There are artificial flowers these days that you cannot tell from the real ones, right? I could buy some, cut them off at the stems, and tape them to the branches of those rose bushes. And I would bet that people passing by at 30 miles an hour would not be able to tell the difference. But, just let someone walk up and take a whiff and the truth would be exposed. Now, is there any harm in that?

Not really, there's just something missing. Something that—if it were there, the whole experience would be richer and deeper—and yes, more profound.

For that rosebush, the flower would have to develop from the inside. Something within that bush would have to produce the bud that becomes the rose. Likewise, for us, true kindness and gentleness wells up from within the depth of our very souls; in that place where God takes up residence when our hearts are ready to receive Him. I can share with you, and I will in a moment, some wonderful experiences I have had in reaching out in kindness while I was in the midst of my struggles. What you will also see in these experiences is the negative side. The side that spoke to continued pain and feelings of being unworthy of God's tenderness in my own life. I believe my progress was so slow because I was fearful and untrusting. Those I drew close to were carefully selected. They had to be non-threatening, perfectly loving without making any demands, and they certainly could not challenge or question my motives. That makes for a short list, doesn't it? As a matter of fact, for a long time that list had only one possibility— babies. That is until "Killer" came along (don't ask about the name, it's a long story).

I discovered how easy dogs were to love by shear accident, and not by choice! Our son Shawn, begged us for a puppy and I steadfastly refused. I never had any pets growing up because my mother hated them. Later, I could not be bothered because they were messy and demanding. I held Shawn off until that fateful day when he was playing near a construction site and found a man's wallet. He came home and asked me what to do. There was $80 and credit cards in it. We called the man to inform him, and he said he would come and get it the next morning. Shawn was so excited, but I tried to prepare him for the possibility that the man may not reward him and that was not important. What was important was that he was honest and did the right thing. He agreed—kind of. The doorbell rang and everyone ran to answer it. On the other side of the door stood a 6'2" mass of a man.

With a huge smile he asked, "Which one of you found my wallet?"

Shawn stepped forward, "I did, sir."

The man grabbed Shawn's small hand and as he was vigorously shaking it said, "You are a fine young man!" And with that handed him $20.

Shawn's eyes lit up, "WOW, thanks!"

Then came the fatal question, "What are you going to do with that money son?"

Without hesitation he said, "I'm going to buy a dog!"

UGH!!! How could I tell him no? So, off we went to the Humane Society to bring home a dirty, pooping, messy, demanding...dog! I was not happy. I'm sure I read my list of demands more than once that day: "you have to walk it, clean up after it, potty train it, and never let it sleep in your bed." Each demand was met with an excited, "I will mom, I promise!"

The next few weeks I considered that puppy my worst nightmare. I watched and waited for Shawn to lose interest and shirk his responsibilities. He finally did, and probably only once, because he was pretty good about taking care of her. But that didn't matter. I sprung into action. After the kids left for school on Monday morning, I scooped up the dog and drove her back to the Humane Society. I was certain Shawn would "get over it." When he got home he was devastated. He cried, but not for the short time I had thought. He cried for three days and was very upset with me.

Finally, I realized what I had done was more hurtful to my son than I had imagined. The love he had for that dog was something I didn't understand, but couldn't shrug off. On Thursday morning, after the kids left for school, I grabbed the phone, fearful that she may not have still been there, or worse, had been put to sleep. When I found out she was still there, I was elated and went immediately to pick her up. I went from there straight to school. The kids were outside at recess. I will never forget the scene as I got out of the car with the dog on a leash. One of Shawn's friends saw us and yelled to Shawn, "*Shawn, look it's Killer!*" I let her loose and they ran to each other. Shawn was crying and laughing and so was I. We had Killer for 11 years, and yes, she messed on the carpet, slept in Shawn's bed (they thought I never knew!), and I grew to love her.

Reflecting back, I believe real changes were taking place when I began to see how I was hurting others. I saw it with Shawn, and I had to face it when Wendy told us she was pregnant at 16. Both happened about the same time. I felt tremendous guilt when Wendy told us. God revealed to me how I had hurt her so deeply and I was learning how to ask for forgiveness. That was something new for me and not very comfortable. Of course, the more I did it, the easier it got, which is a good thing because I have had to do it a lot over the years! But, you know what? "*The Lord is merciful and gracious, slow to anger, and abounding in mercy.*"[3] That has been so true in my life. I have sinned and sinned again, but God has forgiven me and loved me unconditionally.

AN EASTER BLESSING

Another profound experience for me happened about four years ago when I took a job at a Residential Center for kids in crisis. But, again, it was a mixed bag of kindness and dogged determination to have my way. The kids, ages 10-18, came to us with varying degrees of serious issues. They stayed from 2-4 weeks. It was the Centers responsibility, in that short time, to evaluate their situation and make a determination as to a course of action. The hope was to return them to their family. There were many services available to help return the children to a better environment than they left, if that was possible. If it was not possible, they were shipped off to another Residential Center, or worse, if they did not conform—a Detention Center.

It was one of the most difficult and the most rewarding jobs I have ever had. It challenged every negative emotion within me and stirred every positive one. I wanted to love and care for every child that walked in the door, but some honestly brought out the worst in me. I could simply bide my time knowing he or she would be gone in a few weeks, but there was always another to take their place. Each time I responded to one of them in anger, I would hear from God. But I never heard from Him so clearly as that Sunday that I was taught a lesson I have never forgotten.

It was Easter Sunday and I wanted to do something special for the kids. Most of them rarely experienced family mealtime, at least not as a pleasant experience. We tried to make it as much of a home environment as possible, but it was not easy. So, I decided this day would be special. Although it was my day off (and we relished our days off!) I would enlist the help of some friends to make covered dishes. I bought a ham, and left my gracious family for the day. The back of my car was packed with luscious food for our Easter feast.

The meal was wonderful and all the kids helped prepare and clean up afterwards. They were unusually good that day, even Justin (not his real name), who had been having a hard time from the moment he had arrived a week earlier, escorted by the police. He was one of the most troubled kids I had seen—twelve years old, small in stature, not looking more than eight, and raging with emotions. The younger ones were the toughest to handle because they felt so threatened by the older kids. It was as though they were always in a survival mode. Any time they could get the upper hand, they snatched the opportunity. But it was usually a hit and run situation—especially with Justin. Stealing from other kids was his specialty and that day was no exception. One of the boys was upset because there was no Easter basket for him. We knew we had enough, but no one seemed to know what happened to it. Some of the other kids shared what they had and that seemed to satisfy him.

That evening, when we all went upstairs, I discovered the basket in the boy's bedroom. It seemed Justin helped himself to two baskets, and was not willing to give either of them up. I tried to explain to him that he could not keep it, took what was left in it, and walked out of the room. He became angry and out of control. There is no reasoning with a child who has known only violence all his young life. He had a habit of pounding on anything available to him: walls, furniture, the floor, people. But it was not just a punch here and there; it was continuous—and harder and louder as his temper rose. This had escalated into a serious situation and we were not sure how to handle it. I decided to call for advice.

There was always a therapist available to us, if not on the premises during the day, then on call in the evening for emergencies. I grumbled to myself as I headed down the steps. He bolted down behind me with such force that if I had not caught him at the bottom, he would have gone head first into the wall! Was he thankful I caught him? Perhaps in some corner of the world, spitting in your face is an act of gratitude, but not here! By then I was having my own pity party. I thought to myself, "I gave up my Easter with my family to come here and put up with this. Kid you're out of here!" We were both determined to win this battle, but I was bigger and wielded more power.

He spoke with so much speed and force, I don't think he took a breath. He shouted, "You gonna call the police, go ahead call the police, have them put me in jail, I don't care, call my mom, tell her, I don't care, you can't do anything to me, I'm not afraid of you." On and on he went. After I shut the office door, I picked up the phone, and then there was silence. I knew he had his ear pressed to the door to hear his fate. After I explained the situation to the therapist she asked if I needed to call the police, did I feel threatened? *Did* I feel threatened? I rubbed my cheek, in the spot where just moments before I was wiping away spit.

Suddenly I realized this was Easter Sunday! Jesus was spit on, beaten mercilessly, and hung on a cross. We all know how He responded. In a gesture that is humanly impossible to understand, He forgave. That realization helped me to see a hurting child rather than an enemy. I could also forgive.

I told her I could handle it; it would be fine. We hung-up and I opened the door prepared for my adversary to fall through the doorway. He did. Before I could get the words out he began his litany of hateful and angry words. I explained to him that I was not going to call the police or his mom. That if he would just go upstairs, take his shower, and go to bed it would be finished. I began to explain to him the reason I made that decision was because I cared about him, but that set him off again. "You don't care about me, no one cares about me, my dad doesn't care about me, how can you?" I tried to apologize for the entire world and insisted I really did care. I said to him without hesitation, "Justin, if you need a hug, I've got one for you." Somewhere between the pounding of the chair against the wall and the door slamming, I heard, "YEAH RIGHT!" I found myself echoing that response several times as I began writing the mandatory Incident Report. Yeah right, what was I thinking?

The Incident Report—just the facts. No room here for emotion or feelings. Names, date, time, incident in detail, outcome, sign it—finished. Or was it? I listed the outcome as: Justin went upstairs and went to bed. Little did I know that was not the final outcome.

I hated writing Incident Reports; they inevitably invoked the question, "What am I doing here?"

We were a shelter for kids in crisis. Truth be told, we took in the throw-away kids. Their circumstances were beyond anything I had ever experienced. When I would sit and listen to a mother who was just bringing her child to the Center tell him, as he's crying to go home with her, "I don't want you, your grandparents don't want you, no one wants you," my heart would ache. I was a youth minister for nine years prior to taking that job. I thought I was prepared for anything. It took only a short time to realize that nothing I had done or seen in youth ministry prepared me for it. With one exception: I believe with all my heart that the longings of all kids are the same. Their experiences may be different, but they all have the same basic need, to be loved and cared for.

We never know where the seeds of kindness will fall or if they will bear fruit.

Were these kids set apart from the "normal" well-adjusted teen? From the Christian teens I worked with for so long? Did I believe none of *those* kids had experienced hurt or pain, none were dealing with serious life issues, none had attempted suicide? No. I never had one spit in my face, although some may have wanted to. None of them dressed in solid black dredge clothes, had blue and green hair, or body piercing in every imaginable place not sporting a tattoo. But those were the *visible* signs of a kid in crisis. Christian kids are good at keeping their pain hidden under designer clothes and acceptable masks. But, I can tell you from my own experience working with teens, and studies will verify, that Christian kids are dealing with the same issues, in the same way, as non-Christians. The experiences I had for so many years with teenagers from all walks of life served as the catalyst that prompted me to offer that angry child a hug—without considering the possibility that he would reject it.

As I finished my report and headed upstairs, I was drained. I reached the top of the stairs just as Justin was coming out of the bathroom. I didn't know what to expect, but I noticed his whole demeanor had changed. He looked at me and asked, "Can I have that hug now?" I cannot express the emotions that welled up within me as I hugged that child. I wondered if anyone had ever hugged him.

> Do we see Jesus in every person who crosses our path each day? Do we treat them the way they treat us, or do we treat them the way they deserve to be treated according to Christ?

There were lessons for me here. As I said before, a missing piece prevented me from being as caring to Justin as I should have been right from the beginning—that piece was the acceptance of God's love for me. I will never know if that moment in time had a lasting affect on him, but that should not be the litmus test for our actions. We never know where the seeds of kindness will fall or if they will bear fruit. And finally, if other people treat us badly, that should not be the basis for our treatment of them. It should, instead, be our gratitude for God's mercy and kindness toward us that compels us to show kindness to others.

WHAT YOU DO FOR THE LEAST OF THESE, YOU DO FOR ME

I now respond differently to people in my life who may say or do something that is hurtful. I don't respond to the action, I respond to the person inside. I respond to a child of God. I remember that other people are just as broken as I am and they are struggling to get by in this messed up world, just like me. When we are kind to other people, especially people who are unkind to us, we are honoring God. Do we see Jesus in every person who crosses our path each day? Do we treat them the way they treat us, or do we treat them the way they deserve to be treated according to Christ?

Jesus said when He comes He will separate the sheep (the righteous) from the goats (the unrighteous). The righteous, He will call blessed and give them their inheritance—which is God's kingdom. But, to the goats He says, *"Depart from Me, you cursed, into the everlasting fire prepared for the devil and his angels: for I was hungry and you gave Me no food; I was thirsty and you gave Me no drink; I was a stranger and you did not take Me in, naked and you did not clothe Me, sick and in prison and you did not visit Me."*[5]

Then Scripture says, *"Then they will also answer Him saying, 'Lord, when did we see You hungry or thirsty or a stranger or naked or sick or in prison, and did not minister to You?'"*[6] They were really confused. These people didn't ever remember the opportunity to minister in those ways to Jesus and they surely would have outdone themselves if they ever got the chance to do that. Can you see it? They are all sitting at Jesus' feet listening to Him preach and He asks for a drink of water. "He needs water, QUICK! Get some water over here!" Whoa! Get back old women and children! You would see hordes of people scrambling for the water fountain.

"I've got it!!"

"No, I've got it!"

"No, He asked me!"

But, that's not what Jesus meant. He answers them in a way that should have shamed them all, *"Assuredly, I say to you, inasmuch as you did not do it to one of the least of these, you did not do it to Me."*[7] That surely silenced the crowd and I would hope that someone holding a glass of water would have gone to the old woman he trampled on the way to the drinking fountain, apologized profusely, and offered her a drink.

What do many people do when they feel called to show kindness? They find a charity they want to support and faithfully mail their check every month. I am not saying that is wrong, I do it myself, and God expects that of us. But, we do need to search ourselves and determine the motive. If we mail a check to help the starving in Haiti, but are neglectful of our own neighbor because we don't want to get involved, our heart is not where God wants it.

Ten years ago, my father-in-law was diagnosed with cancer. Twice before he died an ambulance was called to take him to the hospital. Neither time did a neighbor come to offer any help. Two weeks *after* he died their next-door neighbor knocked on the door and asked how he was doing. My mother-in-law said, "He died," and closed the door.

Jesus said, *"Freely you have received, freely give."*[8] You have the power to change lives by simple acts of kindness. Certainly it requires risk and could return rejection, but do it anyway. How hard is it, really, to smile and offer a kind word to the grumpy checker at the grocery store? How about that obnoxious guy in rush-hour traffic who tries to squeeze in front of you at an exit? Is it your habit to ignore him and grumble some obscenities as you inch closer to the car in front of you so he can't get in? For heaven's sake, let him in. It may not make a difference to him, but your health will benefit from it. And in the whole scheme of life, does it *really* matter? I ask myself that every time I am inclined to return an unkindness to someone. Is this really important; will it glorify God? If you really want to go out on a limb, the next time someone confides in you that they are struggling, ask what you can do for them—and then do it!

Every single day you will have an opportunity to honor God: at home, at work, in the supermarket, in traffic, or on the telephone with a service rep who's trying to work her way through school and gets you—only after you have been left on hold for 20 minutes (according to you), only after being transferred 10 times (according to you), to the wrong departments, and you're late for work, and the bus is waiting for your child who just threw-up on the carpet…and boy, this is her lucky day! How will you handle it? The kinder you are in the worst of situations, the more God's light shines.

STOP THE WORLD I WANNA GET OFF

The television compelled me to stop writing and listen to the news. Another person killed by a random sniper in Maryland, the eighth in just a few days. A father of six who stopped at a filling station on his way home from a business trip was killed. Today's world is frightening, is it not? Sometimes I just want to say, "Lord, just come and get me now! This world is awful and I don't want to be here any more." Or just give me a place to hide until it's over. Paul felt that way, he was tired and beat-up and was ready to go home to be with his Father. But, he understood fully why God had kept him there. He says, *"For to me, to live is Christ, and to die is gain. But if I live on in the flesh, this will mean fruit from my labor; yet what I shall choose I cannot tell. For I am hard-pressed between the two, having a desire to depart and be with Christ, which is far better. Nevertheless to remain in the flesh is more needful for you. And being confident of this, I know that I shall remain and continue with you all for your progress."*[9] God has a purpose for each of us and it is not to run and hide. He made us light to take into the darkness. To shine for others and to give them hope. Jesus declares our purpose, *"You are the light of the world. A city that is set on a hill cannot be hidden. Nor do they light a lamp and put it under a basket, but on a lampstand, and it gives light to all who are in the house. Let your light so shine before men, that they may see your good works and glorify your Father in heaven."*[10] Is your light shining?

So many Christians today choose to turn off the television when a starving child is staring at them. They are the Priest and Levite who cross the street when approaching someone in need, or they will drop a dollar in the hat. Or they may even go a step further, as I did once. It was several years ago, I was returning home from visiting my daughter and stopped at a rest stop. There was a car parked next to me with a sign in the window that said they needed money for gas to get home. Their two children were asking to wash windows for a quarter. I was saddened and drove to McDonalds, bought lunch for all of them and returned to the rest stop. They were sitting in their car as I approached and handed the bags to them. They thanked me and I went on my way. I was feeling pretty holy right then, as I drove away knowing I did much more than "most" people would do. So, what's wrong with that? At the time, I didn't see anything wrong with it. But now I see what was missing—it's the touch.

IT'S THE TOUCH

God could have made His job a lot easier and wouldn't have had to send His Son into this awful world. He could have kicked back in His comfortable armchair and in His leisure: cured the sick, fed the hungry, clothed the naked. He had the power to do that. But He chose not to. He chose to send Jesus here to physically, gently and tenderly, touch sick and hurting people. Did that touch make a difference? You bet it did. And now God calls us to be Jesus to others—to touch. If you find that reaching out in kindness has caused you to get bitten—often, so often that there is a tiny nub hanging from your shoulder joint, good for you! Don't quit, it will grow back! (Hey, it's just an analogy; I can make it grow back if I want to!).

That touch, that I first experienced through Sister Maureen in Kentucky three years ago, changed my life. It was what brought me into a love relationship with God and from that relationship I respond to others in love. So, what would I have done differently in past situations I have related to you here? Well, for my daughter, I would have validated her feelings of rejection and responded to her pain. I would have held her as lovingly as I held her baby brothers. For Shawn, I would have seen how precious his love for Killer was, and overlooked the few times he forgot some part of her care. For Justin, I would have been able to balance discipline with love from the moment he walked in the door.

And what about the family I took lunch to? That was pretty nice. Yes, but did I really touch them? I handed the food in the window and left. If I saw that same couple today I would have gotten an extra bag for me, sat at a picnic table with them and offered them my time as well. That is touching—that is being Jesus to others. Every missed opportunity is a point for Satan.

I will leave you with this, *"And let us not grow weary while doing good, for in due season we shall reap if we do not lose heart. Therefore, as we have opportunity, let us do good to all..."*[11]

Chapter Six

GOODNESS

"...and what the Lord requires of you but to do justly, to love mercy, and to walk humbly with your God...."[1]

I had a pretty narrow definition of "good" as a child. Do you know what my parents said every time I messed up? The same thing many parents say, "You are a bad girl!" And when I occasionally did something right? "You are a good girl!" Is it any wonder I had such a shallow concept of what it took to be "good"? If I straightened my room and didn't torment my brother; if my report card was acceptable and the Principal didn't call all week; if I wasn't caught lying—I got a gold star and a "good girl" pat—for that week anyway.

So, when I grew up, being good translated into: keeping the house clean, the kids in line, the neighbors at bay, and my lies hidden. I would give myself a "good girl" pat and a symbolic gold star—for that week anyway. But, for some reason, I found it very difficult to keep up the charade. Why was that?

Why did I struggle for so many years trying to be good, only to fail time and time again? After all, isn't being a good person something we can do if we set our minds to it? Apparently not.

I always found it interesting that Paul, such a Godly man, struggled greatly with this virtue. He says, *"For what I am doing, I do not understand. For what I will to do, that I do not practice; but what I hate, that I do. If then, I do what I will not to do, I agree with the law that it is good. But now, it is no longer I who do it, but sin that dwells in me. For I know that in me (that is, in my flesh) nothing good dwells; for to will is present with me, but how to perform what is good I do not find."*[2]

As Christians, most of us really want to do good, but we are constantly in a battle. Scripture tells us why, *"The flesh lusts against the Spirit, and the Spirit against the flesh, and these are contrary one against the other so that you cannot do the things that you would."*[3] The key to goodness is the involvement of the Spirit. The Random House Webster's dictionary says, "Goodness is the simple word for a general quality recognized as an inherent part of one's character. Virtue is a rather formal word, and usually suggests goodness that is consciously maintained, often in spite of evil influences." The old English word, "good" evolves out of the word for God. Goodness is virtue that comes from God. So, when Paul speaks of his struggles, he is saying that he is only capable of doing good through the Spirit, because true goodness is only possible through the originator of the virtue—God. Outside of God and by the power of the flesh, true and lasting goodness cannot exist.

WOE TO YOU PHARISEES

Galatians says, *"Don't grow weary doing good."*[4] People who are superficially good do grow weary. I can't tell you how many times I have heard people say, "I have a friend who doesn't go to church, or I have a friend who isn't a Christian and she's a good person." Really? I would challenge you to search the depth of that person's goodness. "Smile you're on Candid Camera!" Our true character is who we are when no one is looking. We can hide our flaws for a period of time, but eventually a superficial or shallow goodness will wane and the true character of the person will surface.

> "The occasional good deed of the unbeliever no more reflects the Spirit of Christ than the occasional bad deed of the believer reflects the spirit of Satan."

My mother was good at fooling people. I had many people tell me my mother was a nice person. I recall one time, my parents and I went to a barbeque at the home of one of their friends. The husband was a youth minister and a very personable man. He and my mother and I were talking about family relationships, and in the midst of the conversation he asked us, "Do you have a good relationship?" In unison, my mother said, "yes," and I said, "no." Needless to say, he was shocked, she was angry, and I just shrugged and walked off. Had my mother been there alone, her answer would have been the same and no one would have been the wiser. In Matthew we are warned, *"Take heed that you do not do your charitable deeds before men, to be seen by them. Otherwise you have no reward from your Father in heaven."*[5]

My husband has said of a man we know, "so and so is a nice guy."

And I had to ask him, "Are you kidding me!? He is abusive to his wife and kids! How can you say he is a nice guy?"

"Well," my husband responded, "He's nice to me."

I read once, "The occasional good deed of the unbeliever no more reflects the Spirit of Christ than the occasional bad deed of the believer reflects the spirit of Satan." Anyone who tries to do good deeds outside of a relationship with God is making a meager effort that will eventually expose him. Jesus warned the Pharisees about their false display of righteousness, their effort to look good in front of others. *"Woe to you, scribes and Pharisees, hypocrites! For you are like whitewashed tombs which indeed appear beautiful outwardly, but inside are full of dead men's bones and all uncleanness. Even so you also outwardly appear righteous to men, but inside you are full of hypocrisy and lawlessness."*[6]

THE SUN SHINES ON BOTH THE GOOD AND EVIL

A good person is usually steadily good and kind no matter what happens, no matter who they are dealing with. It's easy to be good to people who are good to us. It is when we are good to people who are not worthy that our true goodness is apparent. God calls us to that kind of goodness in Matthew, *"You have heard that it was said, 'You shall love your neighbor and hate your enemy. But I say to you, love your enemies, bless those who curse you, do good to those who hate you, and pray for those who spitefully use you and persecute you, that you may be sons of your Father in heaven; for He makes His sun rise on the evil and on the good, and sends rain on the just and on the unjust. For if you love those who love you, what reward have you? Do not even the tax collectors do the same? And if you greet your brethren only, what do you do more than others? Do not even the tax collectors do so?"*[7]

Jonah wasn't interested in that "love your enemy" message. The people of Nineveh were perverse and he hated them for what they did to his people. He wanted no part in telling them that God would forgive their sins if they would change their evil ways. So, he ran away. Jonah held onto his grudge so tightly that it's doubtful he even considered the consequences of his decision to turn his back on God.

And don't think you can simply apply the law of justice to difficult people. Some people would have you believe that goodness is synonymous with justice. But that simply isn't true. Justice is something we should be fighting for daily. And it is what we seek for all of humanity. We see injustice everywhere and our hearts ache for people who cannot defend themselves against it. But, justice, by definition, is giving people what they are due. Goodness is going far beyond that, to giving to those who are not worthy. Can't do it? God did—Jesus did.

GOODNESS WILL NOT MAKE US MERELY "NICE PEOPLE, BUT NEW MEN."[8] (C. S. Lewis)

There is a book in the Bible that tells us all about goodness and it is a mere three chapters. It is the book of Titus. Paul wrote to Titus to give him instructions concerning Crete. This was a miserable place, a valueless society; full of corruption and void of role models. The people were called, "Liars, evil beasts, and lazy gluttons."

In *The Message*, these are the instructions Paul gave Titus as he was sent to build the newly established Church. They could also be our instructions for how to live a good and virtuous life. *"...not pushy, not short-tempered, not a drunk, not a bully, not money-hungry. He must welcome people, be helpful, wise, fair, reverent, have a good grip on himself, and have a good grip on the Message, knowing how to use the truth to either spur people on in knowledge or stop them in their tracks if they oppose it."*[9]

Then in Titus 2, *"But mostly, show them all this by doing it yourself, incorruptible in your teaching, your words solid and sane. Then anyone who is dead set against us, when he finds nothing weird or misguided, might eventually come around.*[10] *God's readiness to give and forgive is now public.*[11] *He offered Himself as a sacrifice to free us from a dark, rebellious life into this good, pure life, making us a people he can be proud of, energetic in goodness."*[12]

Titus 3 tells us, *"Remind them to be subject to rulers and authorities, to obey, to be ready for every good work, to speak evil of no one, to be peaceable, gentle, showing all humility to all men. For we ourselves were also once foolish, disobedient, deceived, serving various lusts and pleasures, living in malice and envy, hateful and hating one another. But when the kindness and love of God our Savior toward man appeared, not by works of us, through the washing of regeneration and renewing of the Holy Spirit, whom He poured out on us abundantly through Jesus Christ our Savior, that having been justified by His grace we should become heirs according to the hope of eternal life."*[9]

It's all in this book of Titus. The goodness of God demonstrated in the life of believers who long, as He does, to bring the lost to the foot of the cross.

NO MORE MR. NICE GUY

The Bible says, *"And the servant of the Lord must not quarrel but be gentle to all, able to teach, patient, in humility correcting those who are in opposition, if God perhaps will grant them repentance, so that they may know the truth, and that they may come to their senses and escape the snare of the devil..."*[14]

> *Being kind, especially to our enemies, can bring far greater reward than treating them the way we think they deserve to be treated.*

He compels us to do it with the boldness of Jesus, through the power of the Holy Spirit. Goodness isn't timid indifference; it isn't staying out of other peoples business; it isn't turning our back on a lost or misguided soul. Our concern should be for what God thinks—not what others think. In today's world, goodness won't win us awards or trophies; it won't get us a promotion or the "employee of the month" parking spot; and it won't get us a hefty year-end bonus. But, if we're good at it, it will get people's attention and if it puts a few on the "hot-seat," so be it.

> It's Jesus hanging on the cross while you're still hanging onto anger, bitterness, and unforgiveness.

You know how that works don't you? Let's say you and I are friends, I call to tell you how angry I am because someone else received credit for something I felt I deserved. I don't like it because I really have a hidden agenda and part of it is to receive undying praise for my faltering ego. But this person stole my thunder, so I begin thinking of how many ways from next Tuesday I can make her miserable. Then you admonish me for my misguided feelings. Who's wrong—me or you? If you are telling the truth *in love*, you are right on.

Being kind, especially to our enemies, can bring far greater reward than treating them the way we think they deserve to be treated. In Proverbs we read, *"If your enemy is hungry, give him bread to eat; and if he is thirsty, give him water to drink; for so you will heap coals of fire on his head, and the Lord will reward you."*[15] When I first read that, I was confused. How can doing good to our enemy cause us to do such a bad thing like heaping burning coals on their head, and then—God is happy about it? Well, actually, it is believed that the passage may have come from an ancient Egyptian custom of purging sin and evil and demonstrating repentance by carrying a dish of burning coals on one's head. So, by that, our returning good for evil will, hopefully, bring the person to repentance.

There is a quote from Shakespeare that goes like this, "There is a daily beauty in his life that makes me ugly." Do you know someone like that?

That's the friend who smiles and nods at the waiter you were about to lambaste for his poor service, and your friend says, "Oh, come on, he's probably had a bad day."

It's the husband who coaxes laughter through the tears of the child on the receiving end of your hot temper.

It's the friend you've hurt, who freely forgives.

It's Jesus hanging on the cross while you're still hanging onto anger, bitterness, and unforgiveness.

Goodness displays God's intense longing to reach out to the lost. It calls us to a boldness that shouts of God's love, grace, and mercy. It gives and gives and gives some more, without need for repayment. It is selfless, with no need for recognition. It is humility in it's finest hour.

At times the very nature of goodness, as much at it appears to be paradoxical, requires us to rebuke others—to stand in the gap between them and salvation. To throw ourselves over the puddle Satan laid in their path, as they step into the light of God's love. It could get messy, but it's worth it.

AND FINALLY

I will leave you with God's message about goodness as told in Ephesians 2 in *The Message*. "*Now God has us where he wants us, with all the time in this world and the next to shower grace and kindness upon us in Christ Jesus. Saving is all his idea, and all his work. All we do is trust him enough to let him do it. It's God's gift from start to finish! We don't play the major role. If we did, we'd probably go around bragging that we'd done the whole thing! No, we neither make nor save ourselves. God does both the making and the saving. He creates each of us by Christ Jesus to join him in the work he does, the good work he has gotten ready for us to do, work we had better be doing.*"[16]

I'm sure you have heard the expression, "random acts of kindness." Well, my friends, we were not put on this earth to do "*random* acts of goodness." There is nothing random about God's purpose for us. Our good works must be purposeful and guided by the Holy Spirit. Titus 3:8 says we should "devote" ourselves to them. The Psalms say, "*The steps of a good man are ordered by the Lord...*"[17] And it's not always a walk in the park. At times it means upsetting the apple cart—or in Jesus' case, overturning the tables to get someone's attention.

We must ask ourselves, is our goodness bringing glory to God and others to His Kingdom? If not, woe to you—woe to me!

Chapter Seven

FAITHFULNESS

God's faithfulness is steadfast.

I can look back and see how God never wavered in His promises to me. But, they couldn't be fulfilled because of my stubbornness. All of my problems stemmed from my refusal to give my life over to Him; not His refusal to live up to His Word. Before I began reading Scripture I could readily come up with some flimsy validation for my refusal to trust Him. I believed He didn't care about me because He wouldn't change the people who were making my life miserable. I felt He had chosen to ignore my pain. But, even during my darkest times, He refused to give up on me. And He refuses to give up on you.

The word faithful is defined as being, "steady in allegiance or affection; loyal; reliable; trusted, or believed; full of faith; believing. By it's nature it requires the involvement of more than one person. Consider a married couple. If only one spouse is faithful, what is likely to happen to that marriage? The same applies to our relationship with God—if He is faithful and we are not. God is always faithful; it is His nature. Jesus was faithful to His death. What about us? How faithful are we to God?

For me, it took the realization that God has remained steadfast in His love for me, in spite of myself, and that didn't come easily. I have failed Him time and again, still he stands true to His word. The Bible describes God as, *"The Rock."*[1] In retrospect, that is what I have seen throughout my life—that is what eventually gave me the longing to be faithful to Him. As that faithfulness grew toward God, it also manifested itself in my relationships with others.

Paul writes to the Philippians, *"I thank my God upon every remembrance of you, always in every prayer of mine making request for you all with joy, for your fellowship in the gospel from the first day until now, being confident of this very thing, that He who has begun a good work in you will complete it until the day of Jesus Christ."*[2] God has chosen you. His plans for your life have already been established. No matter how much of a struggle it seems, don't give up—he is not finished with you yet. The Bible says, *"Eye has not seen, nor ear heard, nor have entered into the heart of man the things which God has prepared for those who love Him."*[3]

A few years ago, when Marsha and I began to truly walk the walk together, we started praying each morning by telephone, (a practice we continue to this day). We would share our struggles and experiences of the day before. We could see in each other how incredibly God was working. One day in particular, we were both amazed by something God had done and how we had expected something much smaller. I laughed and said, "you were hoping for a teaspoon of blessing and He brought a dump truck!" That is now our standard response to God's continued surprises. He loves doing it, are you willing to let Him?

JESUS—FAITHFUL TO THE END

Now, let's talk about the faithfulness of Jesus. God said to His beloved Son, "Go and save My children"—and Jesus obeyed. He did exactly what God sent Him to do, without question. Daily, He had to choose to obey His Father in the midst of worldly temptations.

He took up His cross, suffered terribly, and died for us. What if God would have reneged on His promise of our salvation? He could have, you know. He was watching. He saw our indifference to Jesus' message. He didn't have to watch His precious Son die, and Jesus didn't have to do it. Why would Jesus walk that dreadful Calvary walk through crowds

> *Why would Jesus walk that dreadful Calvary walk through crowds of jeering, cursing, spitting, taunting indifference?*

of jeering, cursing, spitting, taunting indifference? The weight of the cross brought only One to His knees, while everyone else, except for a few, either stood defiant and unmoved, or walked away. Jesus chose to be faithful to the promise of our salvation. It is a free gift, with no strings attached—if we choose to accept it.

FAITHFULNESS SHOULD BE OUR RESPONSE

What does that faithfulness require? Are we to die for Him? Are we to suffer unbearable pain for Him? For some of us, the answer is yes. Job comes to mind for me. Who among us could endure what he did and stay faithful? Could I? I honestly don't know and I pray I will never have to find out. I am almost tempted to quit striving so diligently to become more faithful (not that I would ever achieve the incredible faith of Job), so my name would not come up in a conversation with Satan like the one that started Job's troubles.

The first Chapter and verse of Job tells of his rich and faith-filled life. It says he was *"blameless and upright..."* He had seven sons and three daughters, many possessions, and great wealth. Scholars believe he was a high official of some sort, although Scripture doesn't tell us exactly. He was diligent about praying for his children and offered burnt offerings daily, just in case they had sinned. Verse 3 says, *"...so that this man was the greatest of all the people of the East."*

Is it any wonder that his name was dropped when God and Satan had this conversation? *"Then the Lord said to Satan, 'Have you considered My servant Job, that there is none like him on the earth, a blameless and upright man, one who fears God and shuns evil?' So Satan answered the Lord and said, 'Does Job fear God for nothing? Have You not made a hedge around him, around his household, and around all that he has on every side? You have blessed the work of his hands, and his possessions have increased in the land. But now, stretch out Your hand and touch all that he has, and he will surely curse You to Your face!' And the Lord said to Satan, 'Behold, all that he has is in your power; only do not lay a hand on his person. So Satan went out from the presence of the Lord."*[4]

Satan didn't waste any time. I can imagine him saying to himself, "I'd better hurry before God changes His mind." So, in very short order he destroyed everything of Job's. The first messenger came to tell him raiders had killed his servants and taken the oxen and, donkeys. Then, *"as the words were still in his mouth."*[5] another messenger came in to tell him, *"a fire came from heaven and burned up the sheep and the servants."*[6] While the words were still in *his* mouth another ran in to say that another band took the camels and killed more servants. Then, the last and most dreadful of news came quickly, *"Your sons and daughters were eating and drinking wine in their oldest brother's house, and suddenly a great wind came from across the wilderness and struck the four corners of the house, and it fell on the young people, and they are dead."*[7]

Listen to the way Job responded to this horrific news; *"Then Job arose, tore his robe, and shaved his head; and fell to the ground and worshiped. And he said, 'Naked I came from my mother's womb, and naked shall I return there. The Lord gave, and the Lord has taken away; Blessed be the name of the Lord.' In all this Job did not sin nor charge God with wrong."*[8] Is that not absolutely incredible? But Job's struggles had just begun.

Satan was breathing fire! He was ready to celebrate his victory over God. He couldn't wait to say, "I told you so." But, God—not Satan, was the one who got to say it. Then Satan had another plan. He went back to God. The first time God told him he couldn't touch Job. *"So Satan answered the Lord and said, 'Skin for skin! Yes, all that a man has he will give for his life. But stretch out Your hand now, and touch his bone and his flesh, and he will surely curse You to Your face.' And the Lord said to Satan, 'Behold, he is in your hand, but spare his life.'"*[9] So Satan went after Job again and this time, Scripture says, *"he struck Job with painful boils from the sole of his foot to the crown of his head."*[10]

How much more could Job endure? His wife said to him, *"Do you still hold fast to your integrity? Curse God and die."*[11] (She was a big help!) But, even then he said to her, *"You speak as one of the foolish women speaks. Shall we indeed accept good from God, and shall we not accept adversity?"*[12] This doesn't mean Job accepted his fate without question. On the contrary, he begged God to tell him what he had done to cause God to turn against him.

At first, his friends seemed to have come to comfort him and give him wise counsel. When in fact, they came with an agenda, and weren't so wise after all. They were determined to help him see the evil of his ways—and they were relentless. "Come on Job, God's wrath came upon you because you have some terrible sin in your life, just admit it, accept your punishment, it's for your own good!" Job insisted, time and time again, that he didn't know why God was punishing him. He just wanted to die, he was in unspeakable pain, and God was silent for a long time, in the midst of his anguish.

> You cannot wait until your feet are held to the fire before you decide it is time to develop some kind of faith.

If you look at the book of Job you will find about 20 chapters and 485 verses (as best I could count) in which Job is crying out to God, revealing the depth of the pain he is suffering. But, you will not find one angry word directed toward God. As a matter of fact in chapter 13, verses 20-22 he says, *"Only two things do not do to me, then I will not hide myself from You: withdraw Your hand far from me, and let not the dread of You make me afraid. Then call and I will answer..."*[13] Job's steadfast faithfulness is amazing! I don't know what I would do if it were me. But I do know this: you cannot wait until your feet are held to the fire before you decide it is time to develop some kind of faith.

I can relate that to childbirth. For anyone who hasn't experienced childbirth, I hope I don't frighten you. When I delivered my daughter, 35 years ago, there was no such thing as the Lamaze method of childbirth. You simply bit the bullet—so to speak. I was 18 years old and alone; my now ex-husband dropped me off at the door. There was some serious screaming going on in that delivery room! The next time (8 years later), I went to Lamaze classes. I was prepared for the delivery, and I can tell you—as bad as it was, it did not compare to the first time.

The Bible says, *"If you have run with the footmen, and they have wearied you, then how can you contend with horses? And if in the land of peace, in which you trusted, they wearied you, then how will you do in the flood plane?"*[14] Remember what

Jonah did when the pressure was on, he showed his true colors didn't he?

Faith develops in the everyday activities of our lives, not in the monumental tests that come our way. We are only able to stand secure in those bigger moments because our faith has been tested daily in small things and we have made the right choices, or have learned from the wrong ones. Living in today's world challenges everything we are made of, from the moment we rise in the morning until we go to sleep at night. Because of that, we could be tempted to say to God, "You know Lord, this faithfulness stuff is hard. You have no idea— You didn't have the peer pressure I have!" (By the way, I wouldn't suggest that!)

No, maybe He didn't. Perhaps that's why the reward He offers to everyone who accepts His call to faithfulness had to be something *HUGE!* Surely, when God was creating earth, he had to have that in mind. Here He is, outdoing Himself, making all those beautiful mountains, valleys, trees, the sunrises and sunsets, flowers of every kind, blue skies, and on and on—it's breathtaking isn't it? Then, on the seventh day He rested and looked around and said, "Hmm—impressive. Even if I do say so myself. But wait, maybe it's too good! They might not want to leave. Then what? Well, that's easy, I'll just make heaven even better!" Of course, He really didn't have to. It isn't like anyone could come back and tell! Or send a post card, "Having a lousy time, don't bother coming." I don't know about you, but I can't imagine God building us a castle on earth while He lives in a house trailer. We haven't even talked about the rest of the gift; about sharing eternity with God and Jesus; with the saints and angels. Being in a place where there is no pain or tears. *Sign me up!*

Because God offers us so much, He expects a lot in return. Does He then leave us high and dry to fend for ourselves? What if you accept His invitation? You call and make a reservation. A few days later you receive a confirmation in the mail with a note attached, "Thank you for choosing heaven as your next home. We have reserved your place and look forward to your arrival. Check-in will be required within 24 hours of your departure from earth. Cancellations must be made 48 hours in advance. Again, thank you for choosing heaven and have a nice trip." Lucky for us, that is not the way it works. He put in place all that is necessary for us to succeed. He sent us the Holy Spirit, our lifeline; who takes up residence in our hearts and guides our way. He has given us Scripture to strengthen and teach us. And He is right there with us, 24/7. We have everything we need for the journey.

THE ROAD LESS TRAVELED

So, why is the journey so hard? He told us it would be. What would we need God for if life was blissful and we never struggled? But, we want the reward without doing the work.

The book of Daniel has a great example of the contrast between faithfulness and unfaithfulness. Nebuchadnezzar was considered one of the greatest kings ever; he was a pagan and an egomaniac. Then there were four Hebrew boys: Daniel, Shadrach, Meshach, and Abed-Nego, in whom the king showed great favor. Nebuchadnezzar was having dreams he could not understand and they troubled him. His own magicians, sorcerers, and astrologers could not interpret them. They insisted there was no one on earth who could. The king was so angry he gave a command to destroy all the wise men of Babylon.

But alas, along came Daniel who said he could interpret the king's dream. By God's power the dream was revealed to him. With great faithfulness, Daniel told the king, *"There is a God in heaven who reveals secrets..."*[15] Pretty bold statement, for a guy standing before a mighty pagan king with a short fuse. But, he went on to explain the dream. Well, this pagan king was so amazed he immediately praised God. *"Then King*

Nebuchadnezzar fell on his face, prostrate before Daniel, and commanded that they should present an offering and incense to him. The king answered Daniel and said, 'Truly your God is the God of gods, the Lord of kings, and revealer of secrets, since you could reveal this secret."[16]

You would think from those accolades that the king's conversion was swift and sure. Not so, according to the very next verses he had an instant lapse of memory. *"Nebuchadnezzar the king made an image of gold, whose height was sixty cubits and its width six cubits."*[17] He built this sky-scraper, and with great fanfare, he gathered all the important people in town to come and worship it. And if they didn't, they would be thrown immediately into the fiery furnace. Well, except for those Hebrew boys, everyone hit the ground! Don't think the locals didn't notice that Shadrach, Meshach, and Abed-Nego were the only ones still standing. They didn't hesitate to run and tell the king. Locals didn't take to those outsiders receiving favored attention.

The king was furious and called them to him. He gave them one last chance to either bow before his gods and wor-ship his gold image, or they were going to burn. But, they didn't hesitate to respond to him, *"...we have no need to answer you in this matter. If that is the case, our God whom we serve is able to deliver us from the burning fiery furnace, and He will deliver us from your hand, O king. But, if not, let it be known to you, O king, that we do not serve your gods, nor will we worship the gold image which you have set up."*[18] So, there—how do you like them apples?

Now, the king was burning hotter than the furnace. He ordered it heated seven times hotter and had them thrown in. Then, to his amazement, they saw four men in the fire, *"Look! I see four men loose, walking in the midst of the fire; and they are not hurt, and the form of the fourth is like the Son of God."*[19] In utter disbelief he called them out of the fire and once more blessed God and this time made a decree, *"Therefore I make a*

decree that any people, nation, or language which speaks anything amiss against the God of Shadrach, Meshach, and Abed-
Nego shall be cut to pieces, and their houses shall be made an
ash heap; because there is no other God who can deliver like
this."[20]

I don't see it, but somewhere in there, between the lines I
suppose, is an exemption for himself. Even though his praises
lasted a little longer this time, we find him backsliding *again*.
Even though Daniel tried to warn him, he just couldn't help
it. He was so powerful and full of himself, he began to boast
about how great Babylon was because of *his* efforts, *"Is not
this great Babylon, that I have built for a royal dwelling by my
mighty power and for the honor of my majesty?"*[21] That was it,
that was all God was going to listen to and in the middle of
his puffed up speech God spoke, *"King Nebuchadnezzar, to
you it is spoken: the King has departed from you. And they shall
drive you from men, and your dwelling shall be with the beasts
of the field...until you know that the Most High rules in the
kingdom of men, and gives it to whomever He chooses."*[22] That
was it. As far as we know, the king learned his lesson and
remained faithful.

Just how faithful were other men of God? Totally and
completely, do you think? Is total faithfulness possible? When
I first began looking at the virtue of faithfulness and the lives
of God's chosen ones who exemplified it, like Job, Shadrach,
Meshach, Abed-Nego, Peter, Paul, David, Abraham, Noah,
and the list goes on—I want to tell you, I was disheartened. I
felt it impossible to achieve such perfection. I was certain
God would always be disappointed in me because of my fail-
ure to be what He expected me to be. Then I looked closer at
those disciples, and a pattern seemed to emerge.

We know Paul continually beat himself up for his backsliding; David committed horrific sins; not one of Jesus' disciples stood by Him when He was led to the cross. When the
going got tough, the tough turned tail and ran. They were not

the pillars of their community. They were the misfits and los-ers. I'll bet their high school yearbooks looked something like mine. "Most likely to end up in jail." "Most likely to join the circus." That is exactly why God chose them, and that is exactly why He chose us—the least likely to succeed, by the world's standards anyway. The Bible reveals God's purpose for using these unlikely heroes, *"Let your light so shine before men, that they may see your good works and glorify your Father in heaven."*[23] If what you are able to accomplish for God were within your own power, then the praise would go to you and not God.

When I told my family I was writing this book, they were all very skeptical. When I finished the first chapter and gave it to them, I heard a chorus of, "Wow, this is amazing." To which I replied, " Yes, it is." But, not because of what I had written. The amazing part is God. They knew I had never done anything like this before; there had to be something much bigger than me behind it. It is truly God's work and the glory and praise can go only to Him.

I would like to revisit Job's story. Remember when God asked Satan, *"Have you considered My servant Job, that there is none like him on the earth...?"*[24] What do you think of when you read that? Perfect? That's what I thought. God said there was, *"none like him on the earth."* Out of all the people on the earth wouldn't you expect, at the very least, a small group of God's elite to stand on that podium alongside Job? Not so, the guy got top billing—he stood alone.

All right, do you have that picture in your mind? Now let's fast forward, through Satan's attack on him, through his friends' lousy advice, through his pleading to a silent God— to God finally answering and it is not a pretty picture.

God finally spoke, "Job...sit down." And God begins ask-ing Job rhetorical questions, a litany of them—as Job sits silent. *"Where were you when I laid the foundations of the earth?"*[25] He reveals all the intricacies of the creation of the

WHY SURRENDER IS NOT A FOUR-LETTER WORD

earth and sky, all the way down to the drops of dew. How about all the creatures that roam the earth, oh wise one? Do you know everything about them as well? *"Can you guide the great bear with it's cubs?*[26] *Do you know the time when the wild mountain goats bear young?*[27] *Can you number the months they will fulfill?*[28] *Will the wild ox be willing to serve you?*[29] "Come on Job, tell me, if you know so much." He is telling Job, "I don't remember seeing you there when I created every detail and I don't recall asking your advice." Then He says, *"Shall the one who contends with the Almighty correct Him? He who rebukes God, let him answer it."*[30] Job, ol' buddy, there is a God—and it's not you!

Job must have been trembling about now. He was shaken from his stunned silence to respond to God, "Hush my mouth!" After regurgitating an ocean of complaints, he was reduced to a trickling of an answer. These are all the words he could muster, *"Behold, I am vile; what shall I answer You? I lay my hand over my mouth."*[31] But, God wasn't finished with him. Max Lucado says in his book, *In The Eye Of The Storm*, "God's questions aren't intended to teach; they are intended to stun. They aren't intended to enlighten; they are intended to awaken. They aren't intended to stir the mind; they are intended to bend the knees…"[32]

Job was just a little fuzzy about who was running the show. I think God did a great job of clearing that up here, *"Everything under heaven is Mine."*[33] God finished laying out the majesty of His creation, in great detail. Job finally gets it, *"Then Job answered the Lord and said: I know that You can do everything, and that no purpose of Yours can be withheld from You. You asked, 'who is this who hides counsel without knowledge?' Therefore I have uttered what I did not understand, things too wonderful for me, which I did not know. Listen, please, and let me speak; You said, 'I will question you, and you shall answer Me.' I have heard of You by the hearing of the ear, but now my eye sees You. Therefore, I abhor myself, and repent in dust and ashes."*[34]

Do you suppose Job's friends were witnessing this exchange between God and Job? Do you suppose they were like children sitting outside the Principal's office listening intently and shaking in their tennis shoes? "All right, Job, I'm finished with you. Now, send Eliphaz in here." Job opens the door, looks squarely at his three friends, slumped in their chairs, looking for reprieve in Job's eyes. But, it isn't there. So, Eliphaz slowly rises and shuffles to the door, stammers to the chair, and faces his Maker. God didn't mince words for the know-it-all, turned suddenly witless, *"My wrath is aroused against you and your two friends, for you have not spoken of Me what is right, as my servant Job has."*[35] Then He tells him, "You better make up to Job, big time, because if he doesn't pray for you and your friends, I will give you what you *really* deserve!"

Now, what do you think? Was Job great? Of course. But, was he perfect? Heavens no! Not one single human who ever walked or will ever walk the earth, except for Jesus Christ, is—or ever will be, perfect. As Christians, we strive to be all God calls us to be and we do fail, at times, in the process. It is in my failings and my adversity that I draw closest to God. That is when I realize most clearly how much I need Him. When I start feeling full of myself, it is that holy knee-jerk that brings me to my senses and reminds me—there is a God and it isn't me!

BUMPS IN THE ROAD

Faithfulness isn't about not falling, it is about falling forward. Let me explain. As long as we are on this earth we are recipients, although reluctant recipients, of the sin-nature passed on to us from that whole garden/snake/apple, Adam and Eve scene. We are going to mess up—it is a fact of life, and anyone who believes they are above such things does not recognize their self-righteousness.

Faithfulness to God is like a series of long jumps. You start out, build up speed, and become airborne. You think you've almost made it. Then—thud! You fall short of the goal because of some lame mistake and hit the ground. But, you're smart enough to know, that if you fall forward, instead of backward, you have actually gained ground. Does that make sense? Some people have the attitude of, "Oh great, I messed up again. I'm just no good. I may as well just quit trying." Please don't buy into that lie. Don't let inevitable mistakes set you back. See them for what they are and move on. God is pulling for you. He is your greatest cheerleader. He wants to help you if you will stop trying to do it in your own strength—give it to Him. Do you have a pride issue? Don't you realize that *even Jesus* knew His limitations? He says, "*When you lift up the Son of Man, then you will know that I am He, and that I do nothing of Myself; but as My Father taught Me, I speak these things.*"[36] To me, that is huge. Pride is the wedge between God and us. Even Jesus needed God to accomplish His purpose here. If knowing that does not humble us, pride is surely the culprit.

> Alcohol was the trip-wire that delivered me right into the hands of Satan.

At the point that all of this became clear to me—what also became clear, was that I had a lot of changes to make in my life. I prayed and asked God to reveal to me areas that needed to change—He did. First and foremost, I knew my prayer life was not what it needed to be. If I were truly relying on God, I needed to be talking to Him every day and I needed to be reading His Word. You can't be in relationship with someone you don't spend time with. I was sincere and God knew it. I had a longing that He filled and every struggle was met with hope. It took time, but gradually (as I suppose He felt I could handle it) He revealed changes I needed to make. He still does. I am telling you these things as if they were past tense. But, I must interject the fact that I am continually working in all of these areas. I believe the biggest change for me took place when I made a conscious decision to avoid situations that were problematic for me in the past. For instance, drinking was a major issue for me. I was able to see that alcohol was the tripwire that delivered me right into the hands of Satan. Even when I began my journey to the heart of God, I tried to deceive myself. I thought I could control the way I acted when I drank. That calls to mind the expression, "the road to hell is paved with good intentions."

I was a hypocrite: I could drink and curse with the best of them and I could pray with the best of them. It took me a while to accept the fact that alcohol and faithfulness cannot co-exist. I'm not saying you should never touch alcohol, if it is not an issue for you, that's great. I can now have an occasional drink, but it is rare.

Another area I had to look at was the company I kept. It is so important to have friends who are on the journey with you. I can't emphasize that enough. I prayed for God to choose friends for me and He has done an awesome job. I now have wonderful friends. We love and support each other and keep each other accountable. We know everything about each other: the good, the bad, and the ugly. Deep, lasting friendships are invaluable if we are going to survive the jungle of anti-Christian sentiment that pervades all of society today. In order for true friendship to flourish, we have to bring that faithfulness—that began between God and us, into our everyday relationships. What does that look like?

FAITHFULNESS TO OTHERS

Is faithfulness something we can reserve for special people in our lives? Or is it something that must become our signature—the essence of who we are? If faithfulness is not displayed in every area of our lives, are we simply a "clanging cymbal?" In light of these definitions: reliability, trustworthiness, honesty, loyalty, and allegiance, the word that stands out to me is integrity. Is it fair to say that a person of integrity would exude all of those qualities? Of course. It is the fundamental basis of other qualities. Without it, trustworthiness and honesty have no place to hang their hat. In *Becoming A Person Of Influence*, John Maxwell and Jim Dornan say, "The bottom line when it comes to integrity is that it allows others to trust you. And without trust, you have nothing. Trust is the single most important factor in personal and professional relationships."[37] Am I trustworthy? It is an important question to ask ourselves. And if you don't have the answer, people in your life do, if you are brave enough to ask.

Integrity is built on the small, day to day choices we make, not in a major event. I guarantee you, if it is not in place when those monumental choices are placed before us, we will likely make the wrong choice.

Am I reliable? Do I fulfill my commitments? The Bible says, *"But let your 'Yes be 'Yes,' and your 'No,' 'No.'"*[38] That sounds simple enough, but it isn't. Keeping commitments and living as your word are not valued qualities today. But they need to be for people intent on living a life of integrity. I know few people who do what they say they are going to do. Those who do are an absolute treasure to me and I work very hard at it myself. Commitment seems to be a lost art. You see the devastation of the lack of commitment in relationships. Either couples are living together, or spouses are walking out because commitments are not valued.

I never learned about commitment growing up. My parents never modeled it, unless being committed to ones own-self counts. I too lacked the willingness to commit to anything. I never stuck with anything that became difficult or uncomfortable. And if I gave my word on something, that would last about as long as it served me, not the other person. I had begun many projects and ventures, none of which panned out. If success didn't fall into my lap, or I became bored, I just moved on to something else.

Today, I take commitments very seriously. That is why I am able to say "No," when I am not able to give my best to the effort.

Living as your word. I mentioned that, but I would like to share more about what it really means. A few years ago, I had the privilege of participating in a three year Leadership Development Program. I felt very honored to be a part of it. I learned a lot and developed skills that have benefited me greatly. There was one thing that was so profound for me to learn, and it is this—the importance of *living as your word*. Just pause for a moment and think about the ramifications of that statement. When I first heard it, I knew it had a deeper meaning than it seemed at first glance. What do we have, outside of our word that forms our essence and establishes our character? Nothing. Plain and simply—nothing.

How do you speak to people? How honest are you? How much do other people trust what you say, value your words, seek your advice? Are you flippant about words that hurt others? Do your words build up or tear down? They have the power to do both. How much importance do you think God placed on words? He *spoke* creation into existence! What does He give us to live by? His Word. Listen to what Jesus has to say about it:

"For by your words you will be justified, and by your words you will be condemned."[39]

"Heaven and earth will pass away, but My words will by no means pass away."[40]

"Whoever comes to Me, and hears My sayings and does them, I will show you whom he is like: He is like a man building a house, who dug deep and laid the foundation on the rock."[41]

"It is the Spirit who gives life; the flesh profits nothing. The words that I speak to you are spirit, and they are life."[42]

By God's Word we know of His faithfulness and love. Faithfulness is an intricate web joining God to Jesus, then to us. It is a seamless tapestry woven with unconditional love. All life is worthy of that love. No life has meaning without it. It is paramount to our very existence and our only logical response is faithfulness to our Creator.

Chapter Eight

SELF-CONTROL

"They stumble, being disobedient to the word, to which they also were appointed. But you are a chosen generation, a royal priesthood, a holy nation, His own special people, that you may proclaim the praises of Him who called you out of darkness into His marvelous light."[1]

Recently, my girlfriend asked me if I would open my house for a Christmas tour, for a fundraiser. I agreed. Christmas is my favorite time of year and I love decorating for the holidays. It wouldn't be much of an inconvenience. Although I decorate a lot, the thought of 100+ women coming through my house suddenly made some of my decorations seem less than acceptable and I began a shopping spree that ended with a price tag of $400. I was aghast and I knew my husband would strangle me with the new Christmas lights that he would now have to string. And if that wasn't bad enough, I was certain everyone who walked through my house would notice the missing decorative pillows on my bed and somehow feel cheated for the money they had spent.

I expressed my disappointment to my girlfriend, but insisted I was not going to spend another dime. God was pressing on my heart that I was out of control. She was quick to say that there was nothing wrong with my borrowing something, rather than buying it. Aha! We hung up the phone and a few hours later I called her back excited, and now content, that my decorating was finished. I stopped at the store for one last strand of lights, only 99 cents, and "borrowed" pillows from the department store! She quietly and lovingly told me I needed to return them.

A small 99-cent string of lights and a few bed pillows were going to be object lessons for me. After a few days of intense prayer, several attempts at justifying my actions, God's rebuke, and my final realization of the importance of self-control in *all* things, I returned the lights and the pillows.

Why is self-control so hard for so many of us, even when we truly long to possess that quality? The concept of self-control can be deceiving. At first glance, it would seem that we are on our own—*self*-control. Self-control is defined as controlling one's emotions, desires, or actions by one's own will. When I try to do that, I inevitably fail. Many people struggle in that same way. Try as they may, they cannot seem to resist the temptations that surround them, why is that? It is because we need God. Self-control is only possible through God. Even Jesus said He could do nothing without God. Thomas a Kempis wrote, "No one is completely free of temptations because the source of temptation is in ourselves. When a person of good will is troubled or tempted or vexed by evil thoughts, then he better understands his need for God, without whom he can do nothing good at all."[2] Lack of self-control—a self-control governed by God, gives way to sin.

Sin is the *one* thing that keeps us out of relationship with God, and conversely, it is the *one* thing that draws us to Him; knowing we cannot resist temptations on our own.

God left us the Holy Spirit to give us that holy nudge every time we begin to stray. I don't know about you, but for me, that nudging can be annoying sometimes! It is so frequent and unrelenting.

"Linda, do you really want to do that?"

"Linda, do you think God would approve of those thoughts?" "Linda...Linda...Linda." I considered changing my name! But, I wonder—would I admonish *myself* if I were left to my own devises? Of course not, I would dream up all kinds of ways to justify, or deny, or ignore my sins. That is exactly what I did in the past and where did it get me?

Think of it as root canal! I'm serious. Have you ever had a root canal done? I don't know about you, but I would rather go through childbirth! But, say you are told you have to have a root canal done. The cost is high and you just don't think you need the dentist, so you go home and perform the root canal on yourself. Did you just do what I did? Did all of your insides react like someone just ran their fingernails across a chalkboard? The thought of that is revolting. Well, my friend, that is exactly what we're doing when we tell God, "I know I have sin here to deal with, but if You don't mind I will eradicate it myself, thank you." Sin takes root deep within us and God is the only one qualified to extract it. And you can be sure He won't offer you any false comfort. "Don't worry, Linda, this won't hurt a bit." It usually does hurt, and we usually recoil at the thought of giving up something we have become so attached to. But, oh the relief, once the work is done!

IT'S JUST A *LITTLE* SIN

I recently had to have a tooth pulled because a large part of it fell out. The dentist told me it was too lost to do root canal (oh, darn!), so he would have to pull it. (Just in case you are beginning to wonder, this is not a chapter devoted to tooth decay. It's almost over.) As I thought about it, I thought of how that compared to sin and why God tells us to be watchful of what we might consider small vices. That would be likened to a small cavity that starts out unnoticed. It grows and festers, and has soon destroyed the entire tooth. There were no outward signs and no pain, until all of a sudden the results of the decay were exposed. Isn't that similar to the way sin works in our lives? It begins as a seemingly innocent thought. That is why you must be serious about the business of self-control, and not be deceived by the world's standards which are not aligned with God's. Scripture says, *"Do not love the world or the things in the world. If anyone loves the world, the love of the Father is not in him. For all that is in the world— the lust of the flesh, the lust of the eyes, and the pride of life—is not of the Father but is of the world. And the world is passing away, and the lust of it; but he who does the will of God abides forever."*[3]

TELLING THE TRUTH IN LOVE

As I began this chapter, I was cognizant of two things: God's call to tell the truth in love, and the possible rejection of some, regarding what I am about say. I struggle because it is as difficult for me to write, as it will likely be for some of you to read. There are even rumblings in my brain of the proper place it should have in the book. If it is first, and you are offended enough, we will part company, and you will be able to return it for a full refund, before coffee is spilled on it, or the dog chews off the cover. If it is last, you will have gotten through most of it before it ends up in your next

"What people most want is not that their consciousness should work correctly; it is that their actions should appear to them to be just."

garage sale. That would mean, hopefully, you may have laughed some, and cried some, and perhaps even saw God in a new light—before you threw the book across the room. (We'll touch on anger later if you'd like.) I pray you will stick it out to the end and wrestle with it, and with God, if need be. It's okay to do that, just don't shoot the messenger.

Leo Tolstoy addresses the need for this wrestling in an essay titled, "The Loin and the Honeycomb, Why Do Men Stufefy (I love that word) Themselves?" "What people most want is not that their consciousness should work correctly; it is that their actions should appear to them to be just. Life does not accord with our conscience, so we bend our conscience to fit life. Everyone will find that at each period of his life he was confronted by several moral dilemmas, and that his well-being depended on the correct resolution of these dilemmas. The resolution of such dilemmas requires a degree of attention, which constitutes true labour. In any labour, especially at the beginning, there comes a time when the work seems painfully difficult, and our human weakness prompts us to abandon it. People have a tendency to stop thinking when it first becomes difficult; and it is at that point, I would add, that thinking becomes fruitful.

Often a man stupefies himself all through life, staying with the same obscure, self-contradictory view of the world to which he is accustomed, pushing at every moment of dawning clarity against the same wall as he did ten or twenty years before, unable to break through the wall because he has consciously blunted the blade of thought which alone could penetrate it."[4]

Sorry, I know that was almost becoming a novel, but it speaks perfectly to what I would ask you to consider as you continue this chapter. Which is—denying we have sin in our lives does not change the facts, refusing to acknowledge it, does not make it disappear, and believing that God doesn't care or doesn't know, is playing Russia roulette with your

Salvation. John, Jesus' disciple said, "*If we say we have no sin, we deceive ourselves, and the truth is not in us. If we say that we have not sinned, we make Him a liar, and His word is not in us.*"[5] Calling God a liar, that is a strong statement, but isn't that what we do when we don't believe Him? What is it exactly, that we don't believe? I would ask you, my friend, to search your heart and determine what you do, or don't believe, about God and about sin.

God is very clear about what sin is. Many things have changed in these last 2,000 years. Nearly everything has evolved into something new, or has been renamed to seem new. But Scripture has never been revised to reflect the times—because God's word is timeless. It is as valid today as the day it was written.

If it has not been your habit of confronting moral issues that are affecting your life—peace and joy beg you to take the step that will allow them to take up residence in your heart. And God calls to you in love. He wants you to know something that will help you take the steps necessary to give Satan his walking papers. As I was beginning the daunting task of writing this chapter, He reminded me of all the ways He spoke to my heart as I was struggling with (and still continue to struggle with) the issues of the sin in my life, and that is the Good News I want to share with you now.

Next to me on the floor is a small, old chair. One of my favorite bears sat in it until it became a repository for the behind of our youngest grandson, when he acts like a three-year-old (which he is). Now, it has a nobler purpose. It is, symbolically, God's chair, where He sits while we write this book. I seek His words and His wisdom as I write. I continually sense Him telling me, "Tell them about My love for them, I don't think they believe it. Tell them that nothing of this world will satisfy their emptiness. Oh, and tell them I am a merciful God and there is nothing they have done that I cannot forgive. Tell them will you? And before we get started could I bother you for a bigger chair?" Well, that was all I needed. That, and Paul's words in Romans, *"But God demonstrates His own love toward us, that while we were still sinners, Christ died for us."*[6]

Although there are countless verses that demonstrate God's immense love for us, none, absolutely none, reveal God's love more than this. It is a pearl of great price, is it not? He didn't put any stipulation on that love that required the death of His only beloved Son. Would you have? Think about it. You're asked to give up your precious child, your only child, for a bunch of losers, sinners, and misfits. When Jesus was hanging on the cross, most didn't even notice, and many, who cried at the moment, walked away and forgot.

Did you forget? I did, as much as I have sinned in my life. And it truly amazes me how much my life has changed. But, believe me when I say I am far from perfect.

"Right honey?"

"That's right," replies my husband from the other room.

The difference for me now is in my knowing God's love and *believing* it. That didn't happen for me until I went to Kentucky. That is when I discovered the love God longs for all of us to know. It is the love described in Ephesians, *"For this reason I bow my knees to the Father of our Lord Jesus Christ, from whom the whole family in heaven and earth is named, that He would grant you, according to the riches of His glory, to be strengthened with might through His Spirit in the inner man, that Christ may dwell in your hearts through faith; that you, being rooted and grounded in love, may be able to comprehend with all the saints what is the width and length and depth and height—-to know the love of Christ which passes knowledge; that you may be filled with all the fullness of God. Now to Him who is able to do exceedingly abundantly above all that we ask or think, according to the power that works in us, to Him be glory in the church by Christ Jesus to all generations, forever and ever. Amen."*[7] Would you take a moment and read that again? Those verses are profound. We cannot—no matter how hard we try, comprehend that immense love of God.

Let me ask you something. Have you ever loved someone and experienced his or her rejection? Maybe a boyfriend when you were younger—or a husband who walked out of your life. Perhaps you tried to love a parent who couldn't return that love, or a child who pushed you away. How about a friend you shared a special relationship with. It hurts doesn't it? Next to losing a loved one to death, the rejection of someone dear to us is devastating. Surely, we would begin a litany of the sacrifices we made for that person.

"How dare he reject me, I gave him the best years of my life, and this is how he repays me!"

"How could she hurt me so deeply after all I did for her."

Are we so disconnected from God that we do not realize His pain every time *we* reject *Him*? Can you allow yourself to sit with that for a moment?

The story of the Prodigal Son has all the elements of rejection, love, and forgiveness. I believe it is one of the most poignant of all Scripture—revealing God's love and mercy. Henri J.M. Nouwen tells the story in a very compelling way in, *The Return of The Prodigal Son, A Story of Homecoming.* I have never read this story more beautifully written. He speaks of how the father wants to control his children in order to protect them, "But his love is too great to do any of that. It cannot force, constrain, push, or pull. It offers the freedom to reject that love or to love in return. It is precisely the immensity of the divine love that is the source of the divine suffering. God, creator of heaven and earth, has chosen to be, first and foremost, a Father. *He suffers beyond telling* (my emphasis), when his children honor him only with lip service, while their hearts are far from him. He knows their "deceitful tongues" and "disloyal hearts."[8] Are you giving God lip service? Paul says, *"So then those who are living the life of the flesh cannot please or satisfy God, or be acceptable to Him.*"[9] You can no more be "kind of" Christian, than you can be "kind of" pregnant.

Now let me tell you the parable of the untidy house-keeper. I have long ago gotten over my obsession for an immaculate house. It is usually clean and neat, so if someone is just passing through, and doesn't pause anywhere, it will pass. Most things, most times, are in their given place. Then there is the every third week—batten down the hatches, damn the torpedoes, Noah has landed! Noah is our grandson, you know, the three-year-old. The world stops, the closet full of toys is unbound, sheets turn into tents, and sticky floors wreak havoc on unsuspecting white socks.

That illustration is how I view sinfulness. I know you're scratching your head, right? Well, hold on a minute. You cannot tell from the outside how messy my house is on the inside. The same with sin, if we think we are okay because our sins are well hidden, I have a news flash for you—God knows. Doh..busted! Is that a revelation? Sadly, I believe it is for many Christians. And maybe that is because we have a distorted concept of sin. And no wonder, it is rarely preached from the pulpit and society has rendered it unrecognizable to the untrained eye. That is why God admonishes us to be wary of the "cunning" and "trickery" of men, *that we should no longer be children, tossed to and fro and carried about with every wind of doctrine.*"[10]

Don't let that seemingly insignificant verse slip by you. Perhaps you are in a place where you have simply grown up in your parents' faith, and I'm not speaking here just to young people. I know many people in my generation, and older, who live a faith that still resembles something they have just *done,* it's almost mechanical. If, as a child, you grew up in the church, you first mimicked your parent's faith. But, at some point you needed to step out and claim that faith as your own—a right of passage. That should have involved a discernment process that brought you to an understanding of, and a love for God, and set you on a journey with Him, on a solid foundation that would withstand the "blowing winds of deceit" that can toss you about like a child. Where are you in that process? You need to know that, because a weak faith cannot withstand Satan's attacks.

Being out of relationship with God creates a breeding ground for sin. But, God says for a confessed Christian there is no excuse for sinfulness. Paul had a lot to say about it, *"For the wrath of God is revealed from heaven against all ungodliness and unrighteousness of men, who suppress the truth in unrighteousness, because what may be known of God is manifest in them, for God has shown it to them. For since the creation of the world His invisible attributes are clearly seen, being understood by the things that are made, even His eternal power and Godhead, so that they are without excuse, because, although they knew God, they did not glorify Him as God, nor were thankful, but became futile in their thoughts, and their foolish hearts were darkened. Professing to be wise, they became fools, and changed glory of the incorruptible God into an image made like corruptible man—and birds and four-footed animals and creeping things. Therefore, God gave them up to uncleanness, in the lusts of their hearts, to dishonor their bodies among themselves, who exchanged the truth of God for the lie, and worshiped and served the creature rather than the Creator, who is blessed forever."*[11]

God is not the warm fuzzy, nor is He the cosmic killjoy, some may know Him as. Many have preached the turn or burn message, and although that *is* God's message, He wants you to know more than that. Unfortunately, as long as we keep ourselves at arms length from Him, we will never even come close. I avoided that relationship for most of my life and it kept me right where Satan wanted me—I couldn't resist his temptations. The Bible says, *"For you, brethren, have been called to liberty; only do not use liberty as an opportunity for the flesh."*[12] God has given us the liberty, the freedom to choose the path we will take. We are warned to not use that liberty for things of the flesh. But we do it anyway, why? Perhaps surrender to God seems like defeat. Maybe we fear that our sins are too bad to forgive—or we're just not willing to give them up. Or perhaps we simply don't recognize them.

MORAL RELATIVISM IS MORALLY WRONG

Moral relativism is not just a term you should be aware of; you need to understand it, because it has become Satan's most creative stronghold on Christians. It is surely what has clouded our understanding and confused sound judgment, and it needs to be exposed for what it is—a lie, simply and emphatically. But many Christians have been it's staunchest defenders, all in the name of tolerance. Situational ethics or moral relativism, whichever term you choose, says that truth is different for everyone—thus, everyone can choose their own values. The problem with this way of thinking is—if everyone can choose the values that suit them, then what would naturally follow is that *no* values would be absolute. Take the Ten Commandments—allow people, *with no penalty*, to choose to follow them or not—what do you have? Think about it. Take one example: I choose not to murder. You, on the other hand, like the idea. You hate my book and ring my doorbell (I don't know how you got my address), I answer the door and you point a loaded gun in my face. Being tolerant, I allow you to "express" your views, after all, you should be allowed to express your feelings, right? *Wrong!*

> *Moral relativism is not just a term you should be aware of; you need to understand it, because it has become Satan's most creative stronghold on Christians.*

If you believe that scenario is far-fetched, may I take you back to 1996 and the murder trial of Lyle and Eric Menendez. Do you remember them? They killed their parents. They were both acquitted in their first trials (they were tried separately). Do you know why? Because the defense pleaded for an "imperfect self-defense" and bombarded the jury with their "expert" witnesses. Now, I'm not going to go into the explanation here of "imperfect self-defense." Though I encourage you to look it up—it reads like something from the Twilight Zone. It was enough, however, to render the jury "stupid." They just couldn't decide. Oh, they knew those boys killed their parents; that wasn't the problem. The problem was...well, they just weren't sure if they meant it! I can see how that could happen. Those poor boys pumped 6 shots into their father at point-blank range. And their mother cowered on the floor while they shot her 10 times, stopping to reload the shotgun in the middle of it. Afterward they went on a shopping spree. Yeah, I can see how difficult it would be to come to a conclusion, can't you? Thankfully, there is good news to report here. There was a retrial and the Judge threw out the "imperfect self-defense" plea. The jury found them both guilty of first-degree murder and they are in prison for life.[13]

A sidebar here. If you have not done so thus far, do yourself and your family a favor and learn more about moral relativism and it's devastating consequences. You can begin with the Internet. There is a wealth of frightening information regarding how moral relativism has seeped into every area of our lives. There is a powerful force at work advancing this moral atrocity, and guess what their number one target is? The minds of our children! But, it began long before this. It actually began with those now in their 30s and, of course, they are the parents of today's young and vulnerable minds. So, the forces of change are moving swiftly and easily to inculcate the most fertile of minds, our children's. I would also recommend a visit to the Barna Research site, they conducted two national surveys that should shake you to your knees, right where God wants you. One response from teenagers, I will share with you, was that 83 percent said moral truth depends on the circumstances, and only 6 percent said moral truth is absolute. Our country is on moral life support, and if we continue to ignore the wolf at the door, we have no one to blame but ourselves.

> *A person cannot be fully in relationship with God and believe that values are subjective and morals are arbitrary.*

A person cannot be fully in relationship with God and believe that values are subjective and morals are arbitrary. Is God really specific about sin? You tell me, *"For this reason God gave them up to vile passions. For even their women exchanged the natural use for what is against nature. Likewise also the men, leaving the natural use of the woman, burned in their lust for one another, men with men committing what is shameful, and receiving in themselves the penalty of their error which was due. And even as they did not like to retain God in their knowledge, God gave them over to a diseased mind, to do those things which are not fitting; being filled with all unrighteousness, sexual immorality, wickedness, covetousness, maliciousness; full of envy, murder, strife, deceit, evil-mindedness; they are whisperers, backbiters, haters of God, violent, proud, boasters, inventors of evil things, disobedient to parents, undiscerning, untrustworthy, unloving, unforgiving, unmerciful; who knowing the righteous judgment of God, that those who practice such things are deserving of death, not only do the same but also approve of those who practice them."*[14] Now, throw in the Ten Commandments and there you have it; sin defined—clear and concise.

I would like to speak to all the sin named here in the context of one area. Because I believe that all sin is the same in the way we deal with it, and the way God can help us overcome it. In Geneen Roth's book *When Food Is Love* she says, "If you deeply explore one area of life, you will find the answers to every area."[15] That has certainly been true in my own life. Everyone has different temptations, different sins that they wrestle with. We could play "name it and claim it" here, but I believe if we take one example and work through it, it will provide the basic understanding of sinfulness and create a longing to be in God's will and say "yes" to Him. A "yes" that will require honesty, risk, and a whole lot of trust. So, where do we begin?

Let's just go right for the juggler, shall we? Let's talk about my all time favorite armchair topic of conversation—sex. I would like to begin with a disclaimer. I know this is where I am going to ruffle some feathers, and cause some to want to engage me in a fierce argument. I'm sorry, but my purpose is not to engage in any philosophical debate. Honestly, I am not skilled enough to even consider that. I am able to sit here and write this book because of God's profound wisdom and knowledge, and a little bit of my own experience and twisted humor. So, if you take issue with anything here, you will need to take that up with God. That said—let's begin.

Sexual promiscuity is out of control. Society has shoved sexual sin down our throats for nearly thirty years now. The fall-out has been devastating, and Christians are so enmeshed in it, they are indistinguishable from non-Christians. I could quote you the frightening statistics on STD's, AID's, abortion, births out-of-wedlock, depression, suicide, drug usage, alcohol abuse, and their relatedness to sexual sin, but my bet is, you've seen them. I can tell you that:

- Homosexuality is a sin; as shown clearly in Scripture, *"For even their women exchanged the natural use for what is against nature. Likewise also the men, leaving the natural use of the woman, burned in their lust for one another, men with men committing what is shameful, and receiving in themselves the penalty of their error which was due.*"[16] A recent study by The National Association for Research and Therapy of Homosexuality (NARTH), has proven that homosexuals can change their orientation through intense therapy. (The information is available to anyone who is of a mind to research it.)[17]

- There have been many studies recently that show disastrous results for couples engaging in pre-marital sex and cohabitation.
- Adulterous affairs are *never* okay, and result in nothing but heartache and pain for those involved, and their families. God must have known that because as much as He hates divorce He allows it only in the case of adultery. Scripture says, *"But I say to you that whoever divorces his wife for any reason except sexual immorality causes her to commit adultery."*[18]
- Pornography, and there is no distinction between hard-core and soft-core, is an abomination against God and mankind.

I could go into great detail regarding the truth of the above statements. But, I wonder if you've heard it all before. What I truly believe is that, if you engage in these activities, there is something you may not have heard before, and that is what I want to share with you. I could use all the facts in the world, facts that can be substantiated, or I could expound on the age old fear factor to try and convict you, but I know I may as well try to nail jello to a wall as to try to engage you that way. I know because it never worked for me.

Now, I do believe that having the facts and the truth are valuable; what I don't believe is, they will transform one's heart. I also believe fear can be very healthy. God wouldn't spend so much time giving us a reason to fear, if it wasn't important. Fear is a God-given response to something harmful. I think hell and damnation are pretty scary and if you are one who does not believe in hell, may I say, you need to wake up and smell the fire! God's judgment is real and severe for anyone who turns their back on Him. But, even that understanding won't bring lasting change. Denial is a powerful tool of Satan's.

Let me ask you something. You either have children or you were one, right? Discipline is necessary in training up a child, but some parents neglect to balance that with love. If a child only knows harsh discipline, is that child going to automatically love that parent? Is that child going to long to follow the instruction of a demanding, unyielding parent? Of course not. I know, I had a mother like that and sadly, I did not love her, or heed her instruction when I was out of her reach. One incident that is seared in my mind is the time I was about 8 or 9. I hid the key to our bathroom because I wanted a safe place to run to when my mother would have an angry fit. One day, soon after that, my brother and I were playing a game and I cursed. He ran home to tell my mother, and I, being faster (fear makes you run fast too), passed him, ran into the house, and locked myself in my sanctuary. I heard their exchange of words, then a pounding on the door and a familiar voice demanding that I open it.

"Linda, open the door."

"No, you'll hit me."

"I said *open* the door."

"Promise you won't hit me?"

"Open the ____ door or I'll climb in the window."

Drats! I forgot the window, I swung around to see if it was unlocked—it wasn't.

"Promise you won't hit me!"

"Okay, I promise. Now open the door!"

I opened the door—trusting. She beat the snot out of me, until I fell into the bathtub.

What happens when a child grows up and is free from a parent like that? You know what happens. Every rule they were taught goes out the window and you don't need a crystal ball to see their future. If mutual love was in place as the child was growing up, they would more readily assume the responsibility of self-discipline. If fear was the basis for right behavior, then it would only be powerful as long as the child was under the parent's control.

Fear is an interesting emotion and for most people that fear comes from a human perspective. So, when we are told to fear the Lord it brings up a picture of us cowering in a corner and God hovering over us ready to strike. Not a pretty picture and it certainly would not be an ideal advertising logo for new followers. But, when I finally said "Yes" to God and that love relationship began to flourish, I took on a new understanding of fear. And it looks like this:

I love God so much I fear hurting Him,
I fear my sins will make Him cry.
I fear He will look at His Son on the cross,
then look at me and ask Himself...why.

Only love can bring you to a place where you long to please God, and no temporal pleasure this world offers can hold a candle to that love. I challenge you to search every imaginable source of facts and statistics available and find *one* that will list negative consequences for surrendering your life to God.

So now, some of you have gotten this far and are feeling pretty confident that you are not sinning against God, no way, no how! Do you find yourself saying, "Whew, I'm sure glad I'm not like *her*." Or, "I may not be perfect, but I'm not as bad as *him*." Well, I hate to rain on your parade, but you're not out of the woods yet. Let's not be doing the happy dance too quickly.

Some sins are easy to spot—they have been well defined for us as the "Thou Shalt Nots" in the Ten Commandments. We have learned to separate what we consider the *big* sins from little indiscretions that can be just as damaging to our relationship with God. There is no impunity for a sin just because *we* have decided it isn't a big deal. "Oh, *that* little thing—yeah, I cuss and gossip sometimes, but I don't mean anything by it. It's just, well, it's the way I am—and you know, everybody does it." In Cynthia Heald's study on *Becoming A Woman of Excellence* she gives the definition of sin, "Whatever weakens your reason, impairs the tenderness of your conscience, obscures your sense of God, or takes off the relish of spiritual things, that thing is sin for you, however innocent it may be in itself."[19] Paul wrote, *"All things are lawful for me, but all things are not helpful."*[20]

Let's take television for example. Believe me, I understand—thanks to the barrage of sexual encounters we witness on every available entertainment venue, that yesterday's sordid, violent, sex-ridden, sitcom is today's "Ozzie and Harriett." But, that doesn't make it right. If you have to tape "Friends" because you can't get home from Thursday night bible study in time to watch it, *hello!*

If there is any confusion about just what is sinful and what is not, God will be glad to help you discern that. But, I will tell you my scientific formula for discernment when it comes to doing something questionable. I just imagine Jesus knocking on the door, you know, one of those unannounced visits. Would I change the station, or stuff the magazine under the cushion, or watch my mouth? If so, then I know in my heart it is not something I should be doing.

The Old Testament said adultery was a sin. Jesus came along and said, *"But I say to you that whoever looks at a woman to lust for her has already committed adultery with her in his heart."*[21] Why do you think He said that? Because every action begins with a thought that enters the heart, and there becomes the action. Scripture gives many examples, here are just a few:

> "For where your treasure is, there also will your heart be."[22]

> "...for out of the abundance of the heart the mouth speaks."[23]

> "But those things that proceed out of the mouth come from the heart, and they defile a man. For out of the heart proceed evil thoughts, murders, adulteries, fornications, thefts, false witness, blasphemies."[24]

It is the hardened heart that sins and it is this same heart that God wants us to give to Him completely, "You shall love the Lord your God with all your heart, all your soul, all your strength, and with all your mind..."[25] "For where your treasure is, there will your heart be also."[26] God knows where your struggles begin, He created you that way. He loved you enough to give you a mind to make your own choices, including the choice to love Him and follow Him—or not.

Satan also knows. He hits *above* the belt, right at our most vulnerable spot. If we are not in close relationship with God, he can and will turn our hearts. He is very seductive and very convincing, more than we give him credit for. We are in good company, on a long list of saints bound for glory, who were hornswoggled by the master of deceit. But, God never intended to hang us out to dry, He has the lifeline that can protect us from sin, but we refuse to hold onto it. Choosing instead, to do it on our own, which is a license for disaster.

We also need to be cautious of the company we keep. Do you believe anyone who lures you into sin cares one hoot about you or your salvation? Do you think they care that you struggle? Do you think for a moment they wonder how you are doing? "Gee, that's a shame about Linda's brush with hell… yawn." If they want anything, it is to keep you right there with them—misery loves company.

You may be struggling right now in a situation you know is wrong, but feel unable to change. Please don't believe that lie, as a Christian you cannot compromise on this. God asks the question, *"Why do you call Me, 'Lord, Lord' and not do the things which I say?"*[27] He has told us He loves us so much, and He wants us to live pure and blameless lives. He assures us He will not leave us to fend for ourselves, *"No temptation has overtaken you except such as is common to man; but God is faithful, who will not allow you to be tempted beyond what you are able, but with the temptation will also make the way of escape, that you may be able to bear it."*[28]

> God sits in His heaven and shakes His head at our futile struggles with sin.

We question the unquestionable and do the unthinkable, just like Paul, *" For what I am doing, I do not understand. For what I will to do, that I do not practice; but what I hate, that I do. If, then, I do what I will not to do, I agree with the law that it is good. But, now it is no longer I that do it, but sin that dwells in me."*[29] Paul is struggling because he discovered the law and in his own strength tried to follow the law. He knows it is the way to live, but can't seem to keep from messing up. Why? Well, he finally figures it out, *"Oh wretched man that I am! Who will deliver me from this body of death? I thank God—through Jesus Christ, our Lord!"*[30]

He has an "A-ha" moment! As he smacks his forehead and utters that immortal word, "DUH." He says, *"For sin shall not have dominion over you, for you are not under the law but under grace."*[31] It is God's grace that will conquer sin, not our own feeble determination. Here's the picture I get when I think of the years of my doing that. Picture this, okay? You're in a river and become panic-stricken, suddenly you feel yourself drowning. Your arms are flailing around and you gasp for air as you take in water. You feel death pounding your senses as your strength fads and you call out to God in one last attempt to survive, *"PLEASE, GOD—SAVE ME!!"* You shout in desperation and suddenly you hear His voice, "Stand up!" You think it is a call like His call to Peter. And like Peter, you respond, "But Lord, I can't swim!" He tells you again, "Stand up, silly!" You stand up and you are in three feet of water! Oh…well…don't I feel stupid! But, you see, God sits in His heaven and shakes His head at our futile struggles with sin, and tells us that is really how simple it is to overcome it. He says it all throughout Scripture; His yoke is easy and His burden is light. But, for whatever reason, we would rather take our chances bobbing around in the water than stand on the firm foundation of His promises.

SURRENDER IS NOT A FOUR-LETTER WORD

That surrender thing just doesn't appeal to us does it? It didn't appeal to me most of my life, but when I finally did surrender, He worked miracles in my life. He changed me into a person I would never have imagined, and gave me joy and peace beyond comprehension. Has it been easy? In a word—no. Has it been worth it? In a word—yes! The same thing happened to Paul. Everything we have talked about thus far is described in these verses. Please read them carefully, *"And I thank Christ Jesus our Lord who has enabled me, because He counted me faithful, putting me into the ministry, although I was formerly a blasphemer, a persecutor, and an insolent man; but I obtained mercy because I did it ignorantly in unbelief. And the grace of our Lord was exceedingly abundant, with faith and love which are in Christ Jesus. This is a faithful saying and worthy of all acceptance, that Christ Jesus came into the world to save sinners, of whom I am chief.*

However, for this reason I obtained mercy, that in me first Jesus Christ might show all longsuffering, as a pattern to those who are going to believe on Him for everlasting life. Now to the King eternal, immortal, invisible, to God who alone is wise, be honor and glory forever and ever. Amen."[32]

PLEASE, COME AS YOU ARE

> That is truly where you start—on your knees before God, with all the confusion, pain, and sin, and none of the answers.

Discovering that I did not have to clean up my messy life before God would accept me was huge for me, and I pray you will realize that as well. I recently heard, "changed behavior is not the root of the relationship—it is the fruit." God wants you right where you are. I have a Scripture verse on a post-it note, on my Bible, so I can see it every day, *"Create in me a clean heart, O God, and renew a steadfast spirit within me."* [33] Next to it is, *"...Lord, I believe; help my unbelief!"*[34] That is truly where you start—on your knees before God, with all the confusion, pain, and sin, and none of the answers. Seeking the grace, mercy, forgiveness, and love that God longs to lavish on you. Don't believe you are too sinful to change or that you have to change overnight. Don't even go there.

So what happens when you are convicted and ready to surrender your life to God? Well, I know what happened for me. I know that seeking forgiveness and reconciliation with God is the first step, and I believe that a truly repentant heart is one that acknowledges that the sin is against God, and there is remorse deep within. God called David to a high purpose, He made him a powerful king and David was enthralled with God. He served Him with honor until that fateful morning when he saw Bathsheba, sent for her in his lust, slept with her, and had her husband killed so he could have her. As much as he loved God he didn't repent in a very timely fashion. As a matter of fact, God had to send a prophet to admonish him, "David...David, what were you thinking?" But, when he did repent, he was clearly remorseful. His prayer was, *"Have mercy upon me, O God, according to your loving kindness; according to the multitude of Your tender mercies."*[35] As bad as David's sin was, he believed in God's mercy and forgiveness.

"...For I acknowledge my transgressions, and my sin is always before me. Against You, You only, have I sinned..."[36] He didn't try to blame anyone else. We're good at that, no one wants to take responsibility for their actions. "Well, You know Lord, if Bathsheba hadn't been bathing in public I could have controlled myself. Don't You think she should take some of the heat for this?"

"...and done this evil in Your sight..."[37] He was confessing to God what God already knew. Confession is not for God, it is to show that we acknowledge it within ourselves. It amazes me that we think God doesn't know what we're up to. *"...That You may be found just when You speak, and blameless when You judge."*[38] David knew he was going to have to pay a price for his sin and he accepted that. Before you acquire a cavalier attitude that says you can do anything you want and God will forgive you, you'd better know that David's life was headed for the toilet when he became self-absorbed and turned from God. God did punish David for his sins. But David never stopped praising Him.

There it is, that is all you need to know to have the confidence to humbly stand before God, confess, and then watch in awe and wonder how God will move in your life. Are you ready? One of my favorite verses is, *"I can do all things through Christ who strengthens me."*[39]

Okay, you are still out there aren't you? I'd hate to think I'm sitting here whistling in the wind because you have moved on to lighter reading. I would like to touch on one more point before we move on, and I can already hear the groans. Which I guess is a good thing because that tells me you *are* still here! Anyway, if you're skipping along enjoying this new-found relationship and your life has become amazing, what do you suppose God wants you the do with that? Yes, that's right. He wants you to pass it on.

More groans! Look, I know we have been inundated by the mantra of tolerance, but God never intended it to mean what we have come to know it as, "judging others." We are actually told not to do that in Scripture. But, this isn't about "judging," it's about caring. It's about standing up and saying, "there are moral absolutes, there are established rights and wrongs, there are no gray areas in God's commandments or the sins He hates, and we have an obligation to share that truth—in love—with others.

If you see a friend sitting on railroad tracks and there is a train coming, are you going to take this attitude, "Oh, well she must be there because she wants to be, who am I to judge?" Lord, I hope not. You should instinctually run to push her off those tracks. Never mind why she is there. Never mind that she may have wanted to be there in the first place—she can go back if she wants. But you are called by God to intercept others who are headed for hell. God said so, really, *"Brethren, if a man is overtaken in any trespass, you who are spiritual restore such a one in a spirit of gentleness, considering yourself lest you also be tempted."*[40] Scripture also says, *"Brethren, if anyone among you wanders from the truth, and someone turns him back, let him know that he who turns a sinner from the error of his way will save a soul from death and cover a multitude of sins."*[41] Do you know the cause and effect of a tolerant Christian? The cause is believing the world's view of tolerance, the effect is our Christian candle being blown out so that our brother sits in darkness. Am I my brother's keeper? You bet! Am I supposed to beat him over the head with my Bible? You bet! Just kidding.

I recently read a response to the following question in a local newspaper on the subject of tolerance. The question was, "Are Christian values and tolerance toward gays, lesbians and bisexuals mutually exclusive?" Although the question specifically addresses tolerance of homosexuals, the response speaks to tolerance in all situations. The response was submitted by Marilyn McDonald of St. Louis. With her permission, I would like to summarize it here. She said, "Tolerance in the traditional sense means valuing, respecting, and accepting individuals because they are fellow human beings. Traditional tolerance means living at peace with those whose values and beliefs may be different from your own. Traditional tolerance differentiates between what a person thinks and does, and the person himself. The new tolerance views all values, beliefs, lifestyles, and truth claims as equal. In the current view of tolerance, you no longer can accept only the person; you must also accept, endorse and promote his values and beliefs as equal to your own. Jesus valued, respected, and accepted all people as made in the image of God, but He did not tolerate sinful behavior." God tells us to love the sinner, but hate the sin. When we give an accepting smile to the sinful behavior of others we are not being the light God calls us to be.

Finally, the world says, "my love is fickle, you have to earn it and you will lose it the minute you mess up or I lose interest in you."

God says, "My love is unconditional, you can do nothing to earn it, or lose it."

The world says, "If you are wealthy, sexy, beautiful, smart, thin, powerful, important, AND have something to give me, I will love you…for a while…maybe…but don't count on it…or me. Especially if you run into trouble."

God says, "you are my Beloved. Period. End of sentence."

The world says, "I wouldn't give one plug nickel for your soul."

God says, "I gave what was most precious to Me—My Son, for your soul."

Who is the liar? Who are you going to believe? Who are you going to follow?

All right, now you're good to go, and God will lead you the rest of the way, and you will glory in the same inheritance as all the disciples before you. As Paul says at the end of his life, "*...the time of my departure is at hand. I have fought the good fight, I have finished the race, I have kept the faith. Finally, there is laid up for me the crown of righteousness...*"[42]

Perhaps a motto will help you persist. I'll share with you one of my all-time favorites. It is that of the French Foreign Legion:

If I fall, pick me up.
If I faulter, push me on.
If I retreat.....shoot me!

Conclusion

It Is Finished

Well, here we are. All finished. I'm a little sad that our time together is over and I pray you have found the time we have spent together fruitful. That is the whole purpose, you know, for any of us to share our stories. The knowledge that others are on the same path offers encouragement for the journey. Paul says, *"Blessed be the God and Father of our Lord Jesus Christ, the Father of mercies and God of all comfort, who comforts us in all our tribulations, that we may be able to comfort those who are in any trouble, with the comfort with which we ourselves are comforted."*[1]

So, what now? If you are convicted and ready to chase after God, you should know that God is going to expect you to do it with a vigor that will attract attention. He wants us to make a joyful *NOISE!* Are you holding back? Let me tell you my last personal story and one that had a profound impact on my life, then we will come back to that question.

Eight years ago, both my parents died. My mother died in January, of heart disease. Because my parents did not belong to a church, the funeral parlor provided a minister. At the end of the wake he gathered all of the family members together—twenty of us: kids, grandkids, and great grandkids. He wanted to know something about this woman he would speaking of at the funeral service the next day. So, he asked us to share some happy memories of my mother with him.

For what seemed like an eternity, there was complete silence. We began to look at each other in disbelief. Each with an expression that said, "Come on, someone, come up with *something*." We each searched the recesses of our memories and pushed through the piles of sadness, anger, and abuse—trying desperately to recall that long forgotten funny quip, or enlightening conversation; maybe a silly habit, or her favorite joke; a special Christmas tradition, or what about the time _____. But, nothing. When it was clear to the poor minister that he would have to use one of his canned generic talks, he politely excused himself, and slipped out the door. Leaving me numb from the experience.

Then, like sitting through a bad movie for a second time, my father died eight months later. The same minister, the same twenty family members, and the same desperate grasp at anything that might unleash a flood of forgotten memories. Instead, we revisited the same deafening silence, which invoked anger within me—anger that shouted at both my parents. How could you do this?! How could you live on this earth for over 70 years, stand as elders over twenty people, and not leave a crumb of happy memories? How could you? How could you leave this earth without touching a life—not even one? Not even mine.

The grief I experienced was unexpected and misunderstood. How could I grieve for parents who left nothing to miss? After a time, I realized that what I grieved was the *absence* of the love I longed for all my life. There is always hope, no matter how old you are, that one day your parents will tell you they love you. I waited all my life, but now it was too late, it would never happen.

That was a pivotal experience in my life. It inspired a longing for two things that I would pursue for whatever time I had left on this earth. The first, a longing for God—that would be the basis for the second, which was to share that love with others, first, and foremost, my family, then, anyone else who came across my path. I was determined that my funeral would be different. I wanted my legacy to be—that I loved that I honestly and openly confessed to others when I failed and fell short, and that I knew God's mercy. And I wanted everyone who attended my funeral to have a smile on their face! A smile that would come as a result of remembering the joy we shared, the compassion we knew, the forgiveness always spoken, the love never doubted. It is a lofty goal, but, with God, "*...if you have faith as a mustard seed, you will say to this mountain, 'Move from here to there,' and it will be moved; and nothing will be impossible for you.' "*[2] Hard at times, oh yes, and slow at times, for sure. But not impossible.

To that end, God has done a tremendous work in my life, but nothing compared to what He wants to do. In many ways I have been afraid to move forward. There have been times that He has blessed me so much I find myself saying to Him, "Okay enough. I don't deserve this—and I beat my chest and repeat the mantra, 'I'm not worthy, I'm not worthy, I'm not worthy.' " To which God replies, "Oh, stop already with the drama. I know you're not worthy. I bless you because I want to. That's how much I love you. So, get a grip on yourself."

Jesus said, "*For everyone to whom much is given, from him much will be required.*"[3] My reluctance to receive His gifts has nothing to do with honorable intentions. It has to do with my fear that God will expect more from me. Just like the

Israelites sitting at the foot of the mountain. God beckons them to come and glory in His presence, and they run in fear. Well, can you blame them? There was all that thunder and lightening, and an ear-piercing trumpet blast, and the smoke and all. And, well, it was scary. So, they felt safer sending Moses. "Man, we are not going up there. You go."

Do you know what their cowardice got them? They spent all those years roaming around in the desert and never made it to the promised land. They fell a little short of the goal. How short we don't know. I wonder if they even cared. Like so many of us they may have just settled into an existence, they became content with, at the foot of the mountain.

There seems to be no doubt that Jonah sat at the foot of that mountain. How much more would we have seen of Jonah, if he would have gotten off his high horse, and down on his knees?

In *The God Chasers*, Tommy Tenney says it beautifully, "He (God) called them to a place—a place of blessings and a place of change—where they didn't want to go. Don't fall into the trap of thinking that this "place" was merely some physical spot on the map...God called them to a *promised place* in Him."[4]

I can relate to the Israelites. I plopped myself down at the foot of that mountain for most of my life. Do you know what happens when you sit at the foot of a mountain? If you sit there long enough you're gonna get pelted with rocks, and boulders, and other "stuff." Maybe even bird "stuff." Being in relationship with God doesn't eliminate the pelting, but the higher you go on the mountain, the less it hurts!

So, the higher you go and the closer you get to God, the more on fire for Him you will become. (That makes sense doesn't it?) On fire is where He wants us, and He will settle for nothing less. Less is what He speaks of in Revelation, "*I know your works, that you are neither cold or hot. I could wish you were cold or hot. So then, because you are lukewarm, and neither cold or hot,* (now watch this) *I will vomit you out of My mouth.*"[5] That's not a pretty picture, and yet that is exactly the action we invite from God every day that we shuffle through life on auto-pilot.

Gain-Carlo Menotti said, "Hell begins on the day when God grants us a clear picture of what we might have achieved, of all the gifts we wasted, of all that we did not do." Being on fire for God beats the alternative!

Come on! Let God out of that box, and let yourself out of the ordinary. He will absolutely amaze you. Absolutely! John Wesley, the founder of the Methodist Church, told why people came to hear him preach in such large numbers, "I set myself on fire, and people came to see me burn." Actually, God will set you on fire, if you let Him. For me, when I first began to long for a relationship with Him, I couldn't get enough. The more Scripture I read and the more time I spent in prayer, the hungrier I became, and the more willing I was to share the things I had discovered. In the beginning, that sharing was done with a select few, safe people, but has since grown to include even strangers. No one has ever attacked me. They may not have agreed with me, or may have been politely disinterested, but I did what God wanted me to do, and I am not responsible for the outcome. Had someone not reached out to me, I would not be able to reach out to others.

My encouragement comes from those in Scripture who went before us. They are incredible examples of your average, everyday, run-of-the-mill, guy on the street—that God zapped and turned into unstoppable warriors for God's kingdom.

Now, how about you? I don't think I have sugar-coated any of the message to *"Go therefore, and make disciples of all nations."*[6] Jesus made it clear, *"If anyone desires to come after me, let him deny himself, and take up his cross, and follow me.*[7] Translated in today's world that will be like being on the New Jersey Freeway—during rush hour—in a rowboat. The world is going to try to make road kill out of you. There is more and more persecution of Christians right here in these United States, and it is going to get worse before it gets better—when Jesus comes. In the meantime, you have a decision to make. And it is as complicated and as simple as this: are you living for this world or the next? We can't fathom what living for an eternity is like, we think it is equivalent to the space of time we spend in rush hour traffic, or being put on hold.

We need a revival! But, it needs to be a revival within our hearts *first*. We praise God in church on Sunday, then the rest of the week we are the same worldly person as the guy next door. Our hallauah within the safety of our church walls, is not resounding in our day-to-day living. We don't speak of Jesus to our neighbor; or for that matter, to our kids, or spouses at home. We put on our Sunday-go-to-meetin' clothes and our Sunday-go-to-meetin' attitude. But, we disrobe that attitude right along with our Sunday best. Until next week.

The pursuit of God is not for the faint of heart, it is not without pain and suffering, and it is not possible without surrendering ourselves to Him. What it is without is—regrets. You have never heard anyone at the end of their life say, "Gosh, I wish I would have spent less time with God and more time making money!"

I would like to leave you with a sincere thank you and this blessing, the same blessing God gave Moses for the Israelites, *"The Lord bless you and keep you; The Lord make His face shine upon you, and be gracious to you; The Lord life up His countenance upon you, and give you peace."*[9]

Notes

Introduction:
1. Matthew 12:40
2. Galatians 5:22,23
3. Galatians 5:25

Chapter 1: Love
1. 1 John 4:19
2. John 15:13
3. Ephesians 4:32
4. Matthew 16:21,22
5. Matthew 16:23
6. Luke 23:34
7. Henry and Richard Blackaby, *Experiencing God* (Nashville: Broadman & Holman Publishers, 1997) p. 77
8. Matthew 6:14
9. James 3:13-17
10. Proverbs 16:5
11. Daniel 4:30
12. Daniel 4:32
13. Daniel 4:34
14. Jonah 3:4
15. Luke 18:11
16. John 5:30
17. Jeremiah 17:4
18. Jeremiah 25:30
19. Jeremiah 25:33
20. Jeremiah 25:34
21. Romans 12:19
22. Neil Clark Warren, PhD, *Make Anger Your Ally* (Colorado Springs: Focus on the Family, 1990) p. 78
23. Mark 16:7
24. Psalm 37:1-2
25. Proverbs 24:17-18
26. 1 Corinthians 9:24

27. 1 Corinthians 16:13
28. 2 Corinthians 1:3
29. 2 Corinthians 4:8-9
30. Colossians 1:24
31. 2 Corinthians 12:8-10
32. David Pelzer, *A Child Called It* (Omaha: Omaha Press Publishing 1993)
33. Genesis 50:20
34. Matthew 27:54
35. 1 Peter 3:18
36. 1 Peter 4:13-16
37. C.S. Lewis, *The Four Loves,* chapter 6, page 13
38. 1 Corinthians 13:13
39. 1 John 4:20-21
40. 1 John 3:18

Chapter 2: Joy

1. Psalms 98:4
2. John 15:11
3. John 16:20
4. Acts 16:25
5. Philippians 1:12-14
6. Philippians 1:20
7. Philippians 2:14
8. 1 Peter 1:6-9
9. Matthew 28:19
10. John 10:10
11. Luke 18:18-23
12. Galatians 5:19-21
13. Matthew 28:19
14. Revelations 3:15-16
15. William Bennett, *The Death of Outrage* (New York: The Free Press, 1998) p. 121
16. Luke 16:13
17. Dallas Willard, *The Spirit Of The Disciples,* as told in *Devotional Classics* (New York: HarperCollins Publishers 1990) p. 14-15
18. Romans 8:5,7,8
19. Matthew 6:19-21
20. Lamentations 3:22-23
21. 2 Corinthians 1:3-4,7

Chapter 3: Peace

1. John 5:5,6
2. Nahum 1:2-3 *(MSG)*
3. Neil Clark Warren, *Make Anger Your Ally* (1990) "The teachings of the Bible regarding anger," p. 115.

4. Deuteronomy 1:21
5. 1 Samuel 20:21
6. Psalm 56:4
7. 1 John 4:18
8. Matthew 6:27
9. Matthew 14:22-33
10. Exodus 14:11-12
11. Proverbs 16:18
12. Proverbs 8:13
13. Ezekiel 28:12-15
14. Ezekiel 28:16-19
15. Genesis 3:2
16. Genesis 3:5
17. James 4:1-10
18. James 5:13-16
19. Philippians 4:6-7
20. Henry Blackaby and Richard Blackaby, *Experiencing God Day-By-Day* (Nashville: Broadman & Holman Publishers 1997) p. 280
21. John 14:27

Chapter 4: Patience

1. Ephesians 4:2 (English Standard Version-ESV)
2. Beth Moore, *Living Beyond Yourself* (Nashville: Life-Way Press 1998) week 6, p. 112
3. Matthew 18:32-33
4. Romans 7:15
5. Romans 2:4 (English Standard Version-ESV)
6. Psalm 106:13
7. Matthew 7:7
8. Luke 12:31
9. John 19:30
10. James 5:7-11 (MSG)
11. Romans 14:13
12. Matthew 10:8
13. Romans 11:33-35
14. 2 Corinthians 12:7
15. Luke 18:1-8 (MSG)
16. 1 Corinthians 16:14

Chapter 5: Kindness and Gentleness

1. Quote by Nancy G. Danforth in "*A Collection of Shaker Thoughts* (Copyright 1976 by Colin Becket Richmond), p. 53
2. Charles Stanley, *The Blessings of Brokenness,* (Zondervan Publishing 1997)
3. Psalm 103:8

4. Matthew 18:23-35
5. Matthew 25:41-43
6. Matthew 25:44
7. Matthew 25:45
8. Matthew 10:8
9. Philippians 1:21-25
10. Matthew 5:14-16
11. Galatians 6:9-10

Chapter 6: Goodness
1. Micah 6:8
2. Romans 7:15-18
3. Galatians 5:17
4. Galatians 6:9
5. Matthew 6:1
6. Matthew 23:27
7. Matthew 5:43-46
8. C.S. Lewis, *Mere Christianity* (San Francisco: Harper 2001), chapter 10
9. Titus 1:7-9 (MSG)
10. Titus 2:7-8 (MSG)
11. Titus 2:11 (MSG)
12. Titus 2:14 (MSG)
13. Titus 3:1-7
14. 2 Timothy 2:24
15. Proverbs 25:21-22
16. Ephesians 2:11-18 (MSG)
17. Psalm 37:23

Chapter 7: Faithfulness
1. Deuteronomy 32:4
2. Philippians 1:3-6
3. 1 Corinthians 2:9
4. Job 1:8-12
5. Job 1:16
6. Job 1:16
7. Job 1:18-19
8. Job 1:20-22
9. Job 2:4-6
10. Job 2:7
11. Job 2:9
12. Job 2:10
13. Job 13:20-22
14. Jeremiah 12:5
15. Daniel 2:28

16. Daniel 2:46-47
17. Daniel 3:1
18. Daniel 3:16-18
19. Daniel 3:25
20. Daniel 3:29
21. Daniel 4:30
22. Daniel 4:31-32
23. Matthew 5:16
24. Job 1:8
25. Job 38:4
26. Job 38:32
27. Job 39:1
28. Job 39:2
29. Job 39:9
30. Job 40:2
31. Job 40:4
32. Max Lucado, *In The Eye of The Storm* (Nashville: Word Publishing 1991) chapter 17, p. 162
33. Job 41:11
34. Job 42:1-6
35. Job 42:7
36. John 8:28
37. John Maxwell & Jim Dornon, *Becoming A Person Of Influence* (Nashville: Thomas Nelson, Inc. Publishers 1997), chapter 1, p. 27
38. Matthew 5:37
39. Matthew 12:37
40. Matthew 24:35
41. Luke 6:47
42. John 6:63

Chapter 8: Self-Control

1. 1 Peter 2:8-9
2. Thomas a Kempis, *Dealing With Temptations*. From his book, *The Imitation of Christ*, as related in, *Devotional Classics* by Richard J. Foster & James Bryan Smith (San Francisco: HarperSanFrancisco 1990) p. 184-187
3. 1 John 2:15-17
4. Leo Tolstoy, *The Lion And The Honeycomb*, as told in, *Spiritual Classics*, by Richard Foster and Emilie Griffin. (San Francisco: HarperSanFrancisco 1990), p. 241-242
5. 1 John 1:8,10
6. Romans 5:8
7. Ephesians 3:14-21
8. Luke 15:17-32 as told by Henry J. M. Nouwen, *The Return Of The Prodigal Son,* (New York: Doubleday 1992), p. 95

9. Romans 8:8
10. Ephesians 4:14
11. Romans 1:18-25
12. Galatians 5:13
13. Menendez trials. Three Internet sources:
14. CNN (Internet Web Posted 2/17/96. Titled: *Testimony Ends The Menendez Retrial*
15. *The Menendez Menace*: A review of Wilson's "Moral Judgement," Ronald W. Dworlien, M.D, PhD.
16. On the "*Stand to Reason*" Website, "A Reason Is Not An Excuse," Gregory Koukl.
17. Romans 1:26-32
18. Geneen Roth, *When Food Is Love,* (Plume Publishing, reissued edition 1993), p. 200
19. Romans 1:26-27
20. NARTH: National Association for Research and Therapy of Homosexuality, Encino, California. May 17, 1997. This was a two-year study of 860 individuals and over 200 psychologists and therapists who treated them; it's data was tabulated by professionals at Brigham Young University. "This research proves once and for all, that the propaganda being spread by the gay lobby in this country has been without any basis in fact, and I suspect they've known it all along," said Dr. Joseph Nicolosi, a psychologist and Executive Director of NARTH.
21. Matthew 5:32
22. Cynthia Heald, *Becoming A Woman Of Excellence* (Colorado Springs: NavPress 1986), chapter 9, p. 98.
23. 1 Corinthians 6:12
24. Matthew 5:28
25. Matthew 6:21
26. Matthew 12:34
27. Matthew 15:18-19
28. Luke 10:27
29. Luke 12:34
30. Luke 6:46
31. 1 Corinthians 10:13
32. Romans 7:15-16
33. Romans 7:24
34. Romans 6:14
35. 1 Timothy 1:12-17
36. Psalm 51:10
37. Mark 9:24
38. Psalm 51:1
39. Psalm 51:3-4
40. Psalm 51:4
41. Psalm 51:4

42. Philippians 4:13
43. Galatians 6:1
44. James 5:19-20
45. 2 Timothy 4:6-8

Conclusion

1. 2 Corinthians 1:3-4
2. Matthew 17:20
3. Luke 12:48
4. Tommy Tenney, *The God Chasers*, (Shippenburg, PA: Destiny Image Publishers, Inc.), chapter 5, p. 71
5. Revelation 3:15-16
6. Matthew 28:19
7. Matthew 16:24
8. John 19:30
9. Numbers 6:24-26

Why Surrender Is Not a Four-Letter Word
Order Form

Book Price: $12.95

Shipping: $3.00 for the first book and $1.00 for each additional book to cover shipping and handling within US, Canada, and Mexico. International orders add $6.00 for the first book and $2.00 for each additional book.

Or order from:
ACW Press
1200 HWY 231 South #273
Ozark, AL 36360

(800) 931-BOOK

www.amazon.com

contact your local bookstore

or contact the author at
surrender_yes@hotmail.com